THE CONCEPT OF METHOD

THE CONCEPT OF
METHOD

by JUSTUS BUCHLER

JOHNSONIAN PROFESSOR OF PHILOSOPHY, COLUMBIA UNIVERSITY

COLUMBIA UNIVERSITY PRESS

NEW YORK AND LONDON

To

E. U. S.

PREFACE

A vast body of literature, representing not philosophy alone but innumerable other fields, has been devoted to questions of "method"; yet only a minute fraction of this literature has dwelt upon the *concept* of method, and then (if I may say so) only with very limited success. The main interest historically and currently lies rather in the exploration or description of particular methods. The present study asks what makes any of these methods "methodic": it tries to determine universal and essential traits, and the nature of methodic activity as such. But it by no means contains all that I have to say about its subject. While designed as a separately readable essay, it is also the continuation of a general philosophic structure with which I have been occupied for some time and which not only bears upon the nature of methodic experience but frames more generic concepts within a metaphysics of the human process.* This book, more restricted in scope than those to which it is sequel, extends some of the ideas which they introduce and makes use of other ideas which they treat more fully. In a sense it is one elaborate

---

* *Toward a General Theory of Human Judgment* (1951) and *Nature and Judgment* (1955).

chapter within the larger structure, and I have divided it only into sections.**

Approaching a concept frontally, away from its major theoretical habitat, imposes handicaps but is not without advantages. Here I have felt it practicable to use "polemical contexts" as the basis for a number of my conclusions. In these contexts, freely chosen, I have revived certain viewpoints which call for serious consideration, and I have dealt with other viewpoints which are not ordinarily interpreted in the light of the issues I am raising.

I am grateful to Joseph L. Blau, Sidney Gelber, Matthew Lipman, Joan McQuary, Robert G. Olson, John H. Randall, Jr., Evelyn Shirk, and Beth Singer for reading the manuscript. Their critical reaction and their specific comments have been of great value to me.

Several years ago, Professor Randall and I offered a seminar on the idea of method. A lively group ranged far and wide, and my own sense of license was primarily responsible for the fact that everything under the sun got dealt with except the main topic. Perhaps the present essay can cancel the debt. But to Professor Randall, as always, and to the students of the seminar, I am thankful for an abundance of good discussion.

J. B.

** The chapter titles of the other books are: Proception, Communication, Compulsion, Convention, Perspective, Validation, Judgment, Query, Experience, Meaning.

THE CONCEPT OF METHOD

I

"The term method," according to the late M. R Cohen, "denotes any procedure which applies some rational order or systematic pattern to diverse objects." [1] This statement must not be approached as if it pretended to exhaustiveness. But since it was prepared for a scholarly encyclopedia, and since it is confidently allowed to stand without qualification, we shall do well to examine it at face value. For it provokes questions which, at the initial cost of some linguistic involvement, provide orientation into matters of philosophic importance. First, what is gained by calling a method a "procedure"?

Is "procedure" a broader term than "method," as it would have to be if a serviceable philosophic definition were being approximated? If we take a common phrase like "method of procedure," one sense requires the assumption that procedures may be subject to any of various methods or to none at all. But just as frequently, the two terms are used interchangeably, and used with equal looseness and informality. And in still other settings, "procedure" carries a narrower sense than "method," being used on a level with "device" or "technique." One issue, then, is whether, by the use of so elastic a term as "procedure," we get the feeling of having placed the concept to be defined into a significant framework preparatory to the making of differentiations. It might well have been simpler and more illuminating for the definition to have started with the ancient notion of the "way." The Greek *methodos* suggests a way followed, the pursuit of a path. A "procedure which applies" would then have become a "way of applying."

Like certain other types of terms, for instance "construction" or "organization," "procedure" can refer either to something going on or to something already available. In the statement under consideration the stress is somewhat uncertain or indifferent. Consequently, the term "method" is also left indecisive: we are not told, for example, whether a method is of the nature of an activity or a rule, an operation or a formula; or whether both of these kinds of traits are required. The same uncertainty, as a matter of fact, attaches to *methodos,* which appears to lay stress both on the way that is there to be pursued and the activity of pursuing.

"Procedure" is interpretable in yet another pair of senses. Assuming it to imply activity, it can further imply either something particular and not necessarily repeated, or something regular and repeatable. It can imply a step, an act; or it can imply a process. Appeal to the latter sense alone saves the definition from vacuity. For consider the question whether the term "procedure" could be omitted from the statement entirely. Could the phrase "any procedure which applies some rational order" be just as well and more economically rendered "any application of some rational order"? It becomes evident that if the addition of "procedure" has any value at all, it must have the value of suggesting the factor of repeatability where there can be said to be method. And this factor is required whether the emphasis be on the "path" or on the "pursuing." A road, a path, must continue to be that road, that path; it must be available and usable; it must be describable and recognizable, even when it ceases to be in fact available; and it must be specifiable if it is not yet available but promises to be. A procedure which applies, a way of applying, is something that can be followed. A mere applying, on the other hand, may be wholly circumstantial or incidental. A "path" hacked through the forest in a semiconscious daze may be expedient, but it is not methodic: the application of order in such a case is adventitious, being a mere fact among many facts, not distinguishable except numerically from other ingredients in a natural complex.

What is meant by "applying" an order or pattern? It is common to speak of achieving or finding or devising an order. In the latter cases it is not assumed, as it seems to be in the case of "applying," that a pre-existing structure of some kind is transferred to a situation where it did not previously obtain, or that it is imposed on objects which it did not previously characterize. The butter-mold, the rubber-stamp, the bottling machine, provide simple instances of applying a given pattern. The pattern is known before it is applied, and the character of its application is readily predictable. There are other modes of applying, by which the pattern or structure is equally predictable in the character and result of its application but less easily discernible prior to its application. The hog-call results in an assemblage of hogs, the erection of pre-fabricated components results in a house. In these cases the prior state is related to the posterior state not by similitude, the similitude of a type to one of its tokens, but through the translation of rules. The pattern that results is a fulfillment of conditions, yet veritably an application. It is safe to say that there is an indefinite number of degrees in the relative fixity of patterns that can be said to be applied, and in the relative complexity of the applications. The application of political and judicial procedures to political and judicial "objects" is more akin to the application of house-construction rules and materials; but in degree of intricacy, it is at a far greater remove from the latter than the latter is in turn from the application of the rubber-stamp.

In the definition at hand the emphasis on application is disproportionate as well as ambiguous. Many important manifestations of methodic activity are inventive, not schematically reproductive; they involve the achievement rather than the transfer or imposition of a pattern. In inventive method, the product is developed, not multiplied. The best that can be said for the universality of the role of "application" is that in all methodic activity antecedent factors are required, whether they be called expectations, stratagems, or ideas; and that such factors must be recognized as antecedent even if they are not only antecedent. In this more general sense, the "application" would be a utilization but not necessarily a recurring embodiment. The antecedent factors contribute to an order; they are applied as knowledge or memory can be said to be applied.

Why does Cohen state that the order to be applied (or developed, as the case may be) is a "rational" order, a "systematic" pattern? These terms, needless to say, admit of a variety of interpretations. "Rational," particularly, has numerous meanings emerging from historical and analytical contexts that are difficult to interconnect. In a brief definition like the one in question, "systematic" suffers from the fact, acceptable or deplorable, that it is so often used synonymously with "methodic." To allow the option that method is the application of methodic pattern may not be wholly circular, but it puts very heavy dependency upon the meaning of "pattern." And if this is so, we are impelled to ask even more persistently why the definition includes the terms "rational" and "systematic" at all. What, in other words, is the difference between applying an order and applying a rational order?

1. Does "rational" mean to exclude "trivial"? Is the use of a butter-mold to shape lumps of butter not methodic? Is it too workaday to merit the name of "rational"? Triviality may or may not have something to do with rationality. But there is no justification for limiting the notion of method to what is important. There are important methods and unimportant methods.

2. Is the qualification "rational" added to "order" for the purpose of implying that the application of merely some order to objects may be fortuitous or unintentional and therefore obviously non-methodic? But if so, the formulation is misleading. For such a point

would be conveyed by the expression "deliberately applies some order" or even "rationally applies some order" rather than by "applies some rational order."

3. Does the use of "rational order" (and "systematic pattern") mean to emphasize that the objects upon which method is employed are already in an order or have some order, so that method would entail applying more than mere order? That anything discriminated as an "object" is thereby acknowledged to be part of an order of some kind is a thoroughly defensible position. But if this is the point implied, the specification that the order introduced by method must be rational or systematic would not have to be included. Method would be the purposive introduction of a new or different order among objects, whether rational or systematic or otherwise.

4. Although nowadays the term is often used pejoratively, "rational" traditionally carries a strong eulogistic suggestion—and probably this is as it should be. But "method" is not the same kind of term. There are methods of proof, composition, social amelioration, therapy, teaching—and methods of deception, evasion, warfare, dissimulation, crime. There are commendable methods and diabolical methods, viable methods and sterile methods; all of them, alas, equally methodic. Where certain types of activity seem to need the description "irrational," there is an understandable reluctance to classify them as methodic; but the incongruity that is felt arises from a tacit (but unnecessary) equation of "irrational" with "chaotic" or "haphazard" and of "rational" with "purposive" or "consistent." "Systematic" activity also is frequently identified with

deliberateness and awareness. In the definition under consideration, however, rationality is something that belongs to the order applied, not to the activity by which it is applied. If there is rational order or systematic pattern, then presumably there is also non-rational order and unsystematic pattern; for in specifying the type of order which method introduces, we are admitting the possibility of a type which it does not introduce.

What is the significance of the assertion that method applies its order to "diverse objects"? Just what the term "objects" is supposed to mean is hard to ascertain. If the term be taken in its familiar sense of enumerable individual entities, the definition becomes implausible: in many manifestations of method the presence of such entities is incidental or irrelevant. A method of inference, of literary criticism, of diplomacy, or of philosophic thinking may have nothing to do with objects in this sense. When "object" is intended as the most general designation of that to which effort is directed, the plural "objects" is not required, and may even interfere with the idea that method imposes its pattern on any "subject-matter" or natural complex. That the plural is intended seems plainly indicated by the addition of "diverse." The definition evidently assumes that method requires a number of "objects" to be "there" for it to operate upon. All methodic activity—indeed, activity of any kind—does imply the pre-existence or presence of some complex; the activity is itself one complex becoming related to another. But the complexes with which many types of methods are concerned cannot be said to be discriminated prior to the activity. (Certain methods of truth-seeking, for example, may work toward the dissection of complexes that are initially gross and obscure.) The qualification "diverse" actually adds another undesirable emphasis to the definition. For even where certain methods do in some sense presuppose antecedently distinct entities, they do not necessarily presuppose a diversity. The methodic process of interior home decoration does, but the methodic process of counting does not.

II

We may turn to an older but more thoroughgoing conception. Bentham speaks both of method and "methodization," and most often of the latter.[2] His principal synonym for methodization is "arrangement." Methodization may be "applied" either to "objects" or to "discourse." No single term is formally used to comprehend both objects and discourse; sometimes "articles," sometimes "subjects" comes near to being appropriated for a definition embracing both subdivisions. But apart from the mere employment of the generic notion of arrangement, such a definition is never actually developed, and generalization is attempted only for each subdivision, Bentham's conviction being that the two spheres of method are "for the most part altogether different and disparate."

Typically Bentham will say something like this: "In so far as in any number whatsoever, any objects whatsoever are put together in a particular manner, by design united to a particular end, the operation termed *methodization* or *arrangement* may be considered as performed, and the objects so dealt with are said to be *arranged* or *methodized*." The objects-discourse distinction is of the following kind: "On the one hand, a group of subjects or objects of any kind, considered as distinct, separate, and detached from one another; on the other hand, the fictitious body entitled a discourse, —a discourse of any kind, a literary composition included,—considered in respect of the mutual relations of which its several distinguishable parts are susceptible." When method is applied to objects, it is always to "insulated objects"; when method is invoked in "the task of putting together the ideal fabric, termed a discourse," something else is involved; but we are not told what. Bentham says that the difference is analogous to the difference between discrete and continuous quantity. In the one case a designatable "number" is involved; in the other, a "configuration, conformation or shape." Hence, in the methodization of a discourse, the use of the materials or parts of speech is not to be regarded as comparable to the use of discrete objects.

As applied to objects, method has two and only two possible forms: "successive exhibition" and "connected aggregation" (or "co-acervation"). Successive exhibition is pursued with regard to "priority and posteriority" (in place or time), whereas connected aggregation is not. These two forms Bentham sometimes calls "lineal" and "collective" methodization. "Lineal" is also called, interestingly enough, "methodization by means of procedure," while "collective," in turn, is used interchangeably with "cumulative." In either form, "methodization supposes a multitude of articles on which, in the quality of subjects, it has to operate; and, in so far as it is apt and useful, it is effected by making such a disposition of them as promises to render them, as far as depends upon itself, subservient to that purpose."

Bentham tells us that where the arrangement of objects is "psychical" rather than "physical"—where we are concerned with the "ideas" of objects, as in natural philosophy—"it is only by means of names, viz. simple or compound, that things are susceptible of arrangement." In Bentham's usage "things" can variously apply to "bodies," "persons," or "substances." But at the same time "things" or "entities" can be divided into the "real" and the "fictitious." A discourse, we saw, is described as a fictitious body. Now since in methodization as applied to objects it may be names which are primarily involved (more generally, audible, visible, or tangible "signs"), and since in this form of methodization both real and fictitious entities are dealt with, the distinction between this form of methodization and methodization as applied to discourse becomes even more confusing than when first stated.

By means of a favorite example, Bentham elaborates his distinction between objects methodized by successive exhibition and objects methodized by connected aggregation. "To physical and psychical methodization this distinction is alike applicable. Fifty guineas disposed in a row are methodized by means of succession; enclosed altogether in a *rouleau*—a sort of extempore paper-box—they are methodized by aggregation and enclosure, or inclusion. . . . In the psychical mode of methodization, arrangement of the names of the objects in a determinate figure, such as a line vertical or horizontal, is arrangement on the principle of lineal succession; arrangement of them under a common denomination, is arrangement on the principle of aggregation and enclosure. The name, the common denomination, is, as it were, the box, the *rouleau,* in which they are enclosed, and by which they are kept together."

Method, according to Bentham, is "the exercise of what may be termed the *tactic* faculty." And the art of method is a very considerable portion of the art of logic. Technically, in Bentham's sprawling tables of classification, methodization is one of "several distinguishable mental operations," such as perception, judgment, memory, abstraction, imagination, and invention. But in practice it constitutes so large a portion of logic, and is "so difficult to confine within any certain determinate limits, that the task of showing what the art of method can do, is scarcely distinguishable from the task of showing what the art of logic can itself do in all its totality." Metaphorically speaking, if logic "were to be termed a *queen,* methodization, method, might be termed her *prime-minister.*" Logic Bentham defines as "the art which has for its object, or end in view, the giving, to the best advantage, direction to the human mind, and thence to the human frame, in its pursuit of any object or purpose, to the attainment of which it is capable of being applied." Its field, "the subject on which its operations are performed . . . is neither more nor less than the entire field of human thought and action." Accordingly, logic and its principal part, method, apply to "the whole field of art and science," but also to "the field of ordinary, i.e., unscientific *thought,* and ordinary, i.e., unartificial action, or say *practice.*" If so, what about the relation of logic to ethics? Bentham has an answer.

"If, in the pursuit of *well-being,* it be the province of ethics to take the direction of human conduct, in that same pursuit it is the province of logic to take the command and give direction to the course of ethics itself." To describe logic or method as an art is not to deny its character as a science. A fundamental conviction of Bentham is that "between art and science, there exists throughout the whole field of thought and action, a constant conjunction: for every science a correspondent art, and for every art a correspondent science."

Bentham distinguishes between method and invention. "Among the objects of invention or discovery, is method: and, when once invented or discovered, it becomes an instrument in the hands of invention, of discovery, and of observation." The relation between the two is reciprocal in a special way. "Method is not the same thing as invention; for, from method, invention . . . as well as the other operations and their correspondent faculties, is capable of receiving direction and assistance. . . . But method is itself the product of invention;—one of the most difficult works that it was ever employed in the execution of." Method may be an instrument not only of invention but of "every one of the . . . faculties, in the exercise of which the attention is employed." And yet, so great is the ultimate importance of method "in comparison with these its associates . . . that they are all of them but, as it were, instruments in its hands."

Three fundamental operations inherently linked together are invention, imagination, and abstraction. Invention is "imagination directed in its exercise to the attainment of some particular end"; or, "imagination, taken under command by attention, and directed to the accomplishment of some particular object or end in view." Imagination is the faculty whereby "a number of abstracted ideas . . . are combined, compounded, put together as it were, into one image. It is combination, preceded by, and operating upon, the products of abstraction." Important to method in the last analysis, therefore, is "abstraction, whence imagination and invention." Although invention is heavily dependent on method, "yet, it is not by methodization alone that what has been performed in the way of invention has been performed. To chance, and to analogy great, also, have been its debts: it has received much favor and assistance from this or that single and insulated analogy presented in some happy moment, by the hand of chance."

The hierarchic sense that is such a peculiar gift in Bentham lends charm to his opinions about the nature of method. His ideas about the purview of logic and ethics, or about the relation between science and art, are stimulating. His metaphorical prowess belongs to an old and strong philosophic tradition that reaches into the twentieth century. We shall not evaluate these or other Benthamite ideas but confine our critique to the definitions and distinctions most pertinent to the present study.

III

Can we justifiably say that method is at least "arrangement," whatever else it may be? It seems plain that a
method of constructing machines or a method of cook-
ery requires the combination of elements or materials.
But in a method of observation or a method of political
action we would be hard put, not only to say in what
sense an arrangement takes place, but to say what the
elements are that could be arranged. If "arrangement"
meant the bringing into being of an intended order
of some kind, the claim for its universality would be
stronger, though we should have departed considerably
from Bentham's own usage. Bentham habitually thinks
of arrangement in terms of "putting together," as if the
methodic contribution to order always consisted in the
imposition of regularity, familiarity, and predictability
on near-chaos. We might, of course, stretch "putting together" to signify the union of all the conditions and
properties emerging from what we do: for instance, the
"combination" of light and dark patches and pointer
readings in an observational process, or the "combination" of speeches, social incidents, newspaper reports,
and conversations that are said to enter into political
action. Bentham does not distinguish between the ar-

rangement of elements or objects that are reckoned as such, and the arrangement of our own resources in methodic activity. If it is straining usage to say that we "arrange" attention, vision, manual prehension, abstraction, and bodily movement, it is certainly no more of a strain than to say that we "arrange" persons, social forces, traditions, and physical events.

It seems possible, moreover, to think of arrangement as deliberate and yet as non-methodic. Suppose a man busily engaged in the calculation of his income tax. He hears the doorbell ring, and he fears that a visitor may talk to him about his financial affairs. He hastily opens the drawers of his desk, stuffing them with records, schedules, and forms, even managing to put the larger papers into the larger drawers and the smaller papers into the smaller. The action is an arrangement: one destination for the papers is chosen above another, the drawers are preferred to the wastebasket. Can the action be regarded as methodic? It is purposive but isolated, and irrelevant to the tax calculation process which had originally been chosen as the framework of operations. It is purposive as a response to an unforeseen event. This in itself would not make it non-methodic. But the order within which it now proceeds is improvised. The arrangement is an action that is literally planned but is not part of an order that was intended as reproducible.

In Bentham, as in widespread later usage, a method is "applied." Objects are "by design directed to a particular end." Method on the one side, objects on the other, are initially independent of one another. Both are initially determinate and self-sufficient. Method can be applied or not applied, as we choose, and it can be applied to any set of objects which yields the prospect of being arranged in accordance with a given purpose. The objects are what they are, whether methodized or unmethodized. Where methodized, they are "disposed" toward or made "subservient to" the "end in view" (a characteristic Benthamite phrase). Bentham never raises the question whether a particular group of objects may modify the method being applied to them. Conversely, the sole change that he acknowledges in objects as a result of methodization is in the pattern of their grouping—either succession or aggregation, lineal or collective grouping. Gross qualitative alterations other than these, or consequent upon these, are given no place in the account. Nor does the thought occur that the altered group may entail alteration in the individuals as grouped. Actually, the patterning, the succession or aggregation, is assumed to have a "fictitious" status, and is regarded by Bentham as wholly derivative in its being from prior "real" entities.

Bentham thinks of method not only as repeatable activity but as predictable in its result. The failure to see that these are two quite different traits causes no end of trouble. The deliberate juxtaposition of the two is a slightly different but equally substantial error. Method, we have seen, necessarily implies repeatability: methodic practice limited to one possible occasion is a contradiction. But one and the same methodic process may have significantly different results in the course of its repetition. In some methods a specific kind of result is predictable; in others it is not. For some methods are modes of regularization (or standardization), while others are modes of exploration. In principle, a generic result can always be formulated for any method. But a method of making chairs achieves products whose relative similarity to each other is the greater in proportion to the degree of fidelity in the employment of the method; whereas a method of composing music or a method of physiological inquiry may (hopefully) result in a product that is as significant for its uniqueness as for its archetypal character. In the latter methods a type of activity is specifically consummated, each consummation augmenting the value of the activity, and each further instance of the activity pointing to another possibly unprecedented consummation. Regulatory method is most relevant in technology and in various forms of social policy; exploratory method is most relevant in theoretical, artistic, and moral invention. When Bentham says that "from method, invention . . . is capable of receiving direction and assistance," his meaning is that standardization can affect and guide exploration. By itself this is hardly unreasonable. The mischief lies in tacitly identifying all methodization with standardization; in not perceiving that method as such can be inventive, and therefore little concerned with imposing prepared patterns. Everyday usage is inclined to make the same identification as Bentham does: to call someone "methodic" is to stress regularity and predictability in his conduct. Accordingly, "methodic" in its cultural import wavers uncertainly on a border between the contexts of praise and contempt.

To be concerned primarily with regularizing the irregular or the unregulated is to conceive of method as admonitory, preventive, and remedial. The particular light in which a conception of method is framed will depend largely upon the conflicting alternatives with which we think method is faced. In a certain light the alternatives may be, on the one hand, slow, steady, efficient, conservative routine; on the other, precarious, risky, brilliant promise. In the world as Bentham sees it, the chief alternatives for human purpose are randomness and prudence. Method is the strategic dissemination of prudence. It is not a repeatable process that seeks to arrive at the new, but a repeatable process that seeks to rectify the old. Its function is to extend the tried, to avoid lapse into the untried. This spirit of dispositional sobriety permeates Bentham's illustrations for both of his grand subdivisions of method—method as applied to objects and method as applied to discourse. Consider, for example, Rule I for "the performance of methodization by successive exhibition" (of objects or names of objects) : "When two words present themselves together for exposition, examine and observe whether there be not between them such a relation, that one of them, and that one alone, is capable of being explained, while the other remains unexplained and not understood; if so, be careful that the explanation given of that one shall precede the explanation given of the other." This is followed by Reason 1: "Brought to view before the explanation, the as yet unexplained article is brought to view without explanation; but if, without explanation, it can be understood, the explanation is of no use."

This rule for methodological health has its parallel in the realm of "discourse." In spite of his emphasis on "putting together," Bentham is scarcely concerned with method as a way of developing new discourse. This function presumably belongs to invention, and method is in effect a benevolent despot preserving and fostering essential order. Behold a diagnosis of conditions which call for the application of method: "A set of incidents to which discourse of all kinds stands exposed, are certain vices or imperfections which, in every shape, it is liable to labour under. 1. Superfluity by irrelevancy; 2. Superfluity by repetition *in terminis;* 3. Superfluity by virtual repetition; 4. Verbosity; 5. Scantiness; 6. Inconsistency, including self-contradiction; 7. Ambiguity; 8. Obscurity; 9. Confusedness; 10. Desultoriness." Sometimes Bentham's forthright classifications call to mind the tables of virtue and vice in historical moralities. The uncompromising divisions, the clear separations, the succinctness of policy seem to exemplify the best methodic spirit, until a longer view and a little more probing show how lean and dry they are in the vast world of methodic possibility.

In the metaphysical individualism of "real entities," the "physical" and "psychical" objects to which method is applied are "considered as distinct, separate, and detached from one another." There is a sense in which this working assumption is unexceptionable. One function of scientific or philosophic inquiry is to ascertain relatedness among complexes, where originally no relatedness was known. The complexes, merely as discriminable, were originally "distinct" and "detached" from one another, relative to the ensuing inquiry. But even in such a case, the purpose of the inquiry and the bent of the method employed is not, as Bentham supposes, to arrange a grouping for the distinct complexes, but to discover or posit an order in which they are seen not to be distinct. And what about those phases of inquiry directed toward discovering differences and making distinctions instead of combining and grouping? Here Bentham's account is even more inadequate. For a scientific or philosophic method may start with complexes in which the subordinate components or relations have not been discovered. Such a method does not initially address itself to distinct objects but instead terminates in an emphasis on (relative) distinctness.

There is another difficulty in the assumption that objects are (or are "considered as") insulated and detached prior to methodization. Why should detached objects be brought together at all? The occasion for grouping may be chance impulse or a mere desire to get something done. But the grounds for grouping must at least in part be actual family relatedness of some kind. The junction of any two objects or signs requires the assumption of potentiality in them. Minimal common properties must be present, on which expectation is based. Otherwise all methodic activity would consist in arbitrary combination, effected for the satisfaction of an arbitrary purpose. There are two reasons why this cannot be. First, a combination that would be purely arbitrary would be purely spontaneous or whimsical—any possible choice would be indifferently likely—and activity of this kind, whatever else it would be or however significant it might turn out to be, could not be called methodic. Purely arbitrary choice or designation of objects is not consistent with projected satisfaction of a design. Second, the properties and potentialities of natural complexes will not permit pure arbitrariness in their selection and arrangement. They will not even permit selectors and arrangers to be as stupid as they would like to be. The very notion of an existing complex implies limits to action, declaration, and contrivance. Even daydreaming deals with objects whose traits have been determinately wrought by genetic and social influence.

Bentham's view of method (or methodization) as a "mental operation" and "mental faculty" (he also speaks of "operations of the body") has peculiar consequences. For he also wishes to regard method as an "art." Presumably it is the art of conducting an operation of a certain type, namely, arrangement. But we must ask some questions. Can we, analogously, speak of the art of abstraction? It would seem so. Or the art of memory? No doubt. By the time we get to this phrase, however, we acquire the vague but tenacious feeling that the term "art" is taking on a different sense. And when we go farther down the list of Bentham's "mental operations" and speak of the art of imagination, the phrase has an awkward ring. For we must surely prefer to think that imagination underlies all art, and all science as well; that it is a primordial power and not a specific realm or medium. And when Bentham speaks of the "art of invention," the phrase really arouses strange feelings. Invention being indeed "imagination directed in its exercise to the attainment of some particular end"—not just a compounding of abstracted ideas, but a process wherein "such compounds are formed as are *new*"—the phrase mirrors a bad confusion. If "invention" were fabrication in some narrow and customary sense, there might be no difficulty. But if invention is inventiveness, the quest for the new in any humane respect, as Bentham's formulation definitely suggests, then it is as confusing to speak of "the art of inventiveness" as of "the art of having the power to make," which is absurd, or "the art of making," which is equivalent to "the art of art."

Bentham discriminates more "operations" than do most other philosophers. Nevertheless he is content to cram them all into the classes "mental" and "physical." Methodization, invention, and communication, which are assigned to the "mental," actually fit into neither class. They are "operations" in a sense quite different from that in which perceiving and remembering or walking and talking are supposed to be. Nor can they be explained as a combination of the two classes—whatever that would be. Their scope is broad; the number of variables in their makeup is large. To call them "human" operations would be better, but a little too loose in the absence of theoretic explanation. To call them "experiential" operations would also be better, but equally unsatisfying apart from a thoroughgoing analysis of experience. Even so, it is easy to see that for methodization, invention, and communication, the term "operations" is far less adequate than it is for other members of their "class."

Let us reflect now on Bentham's distinction between method as applied to objects and method as applied to discourse. The distinction is meagerly drawn—and volubly insisted upon. Although it is impossible to do more than conjecture what Bentham is driving at, the results may be instructive. The problem is the greater because within the scope of "objects" Bentham includes ideas, words, and signs in general ("psychical objects").

For if method as applied to objects includes arrangements of words, what is being arranged when method is applied to "discourse"? We have seen that illustrations supplied by Bentham for both realms deal with verbal materials. Under what conditions, then, are words treated as discourse ("discursively," we shall say), and under what conditions as objects ("non-discursively")? Let us try two ways of construing and stating the distinction.

1. Are words treated *non-discursively,* or as "discrete objects," when they are subject to addition, subtraction, replacement, or alteration without affecting the character of the whole of which they are parts? And are words treated *discursively* when they are considered solely in their effect upon the character of the whole (the "configuration") of which they are parts? In accordance with this principle of distinction, and making use of Bentham's own subjects of illustration, we should be able to say that defining or explaining a series of words successively may be done in different ways, adding, subtracting, or changing words, without affecting the given enterprise of explanation as a whole; whereas introducing verbal economy in place of verbal superfluity cannot be done without affecting the enterprise as a whole. The trouble with this is simply that there *are* cases of successive definition or explanation where the deliberate change or elimination of a word can affect the character of the whole: for instance, various legal, mathematical, or philosophic structures. And there are cases of change from superfluity to economy where there is no reason to believe that the character of the whole is in the least affected—for instance, in the

literary framing of certain statutes, proofs, and view-points within the very same areas of law, mathematics, and philosophy, respectively.

2. Is an arrangement of words *non-discursive* if it is primarily concerned with its ultimate relation to "real entities"? Is it *discursive* if it is concerned primarily with "communication"? From this point of view, the difference would be functional, emerging out of the purposes for which the arrangement of words is intended. Perhaps the former function should be called designative and the latter rhetorical. One function presumably arranges words for the promotion of inquiry; the other, for the promotion of conviction. One produces a series of formulae or a sequence of class-names; the other, a "configuration, conformation or shape." One aims to lead us to real entities; the other aims to persuade or to please or to embellish verbally, whether in fidelity to the real or not. (It should be noted that any limitation of "discourse" to non-scientific or "literary" composition in the narrow sense of the term is foreign to Bentham, who thinks of a discourse as a "discourse of *any* kind, a literary composition *included*" [italics added], and who typically illustrates by saying, "take a discourse having for its field any portion of the field of Natural History.")

But interpretation 2 has its difficulties as well. For (*a*) how can a series of denominations or formulae lead us to real entities except by communicating the properties of these entities as effectively as possible? Do formulae convey meaning less than do news reports, poems, or myths? Are not all signs and sign-arrangements employed to communicate? Designative methodization must be communicative in its very essence, even if not all forms of communication are designative. Thus within "discursive" arrangement further distinctions must be made. Communicative efficacy must be sharply distinguished from rhetorical technique, and conviction from entertainment. Yet rhetorical technique and entertainment value in whatever degree may likewise belong to any word-arrangement. The idea that a word-arrangement largely depends for its properties upon a more comprehensive order of which it is necessarily part is hardly to be found in Bentham. (In all likelihood we should not have reached this hypothetical stage at all if we had consented to be hindered by the restrictive way in which Bentham thinks of communication—"speaking, writing, and pantomime.")

And (b) why is a word-arrangement that is designed to persuade or please necessarily more of a "configuration" than one designed to affirm or record? Arrangement as such would seem to imply configuration. And if so, what does it mean any longer to say that nondiscursive arrangement of words considers its objects as distinct, separate, or detached? Must not discursive arrangement also begin with the unarranged? The elements begun with may not be the ultimate entities posited by Bentham, but they are elements in the sense of pre-methodic materials: in whatever way they may have been arranged previously, they are unarranged relative to the methodic prospect in store. Every arrangement is a whole with parts. Nor can a discourse differ from a non-discursive arrangement so far as integrity is concerned. One cannot be indivisible and the other divisible. Both have come into being. A structure that was actually indivisible would not be constructible either. Nor would it be subject to methodic remedy. Remedy consists not in totally damning or approving a configuration, but in correcting a particular (partial) defect or malfunction.

We turn to Bentham's more special distinction between two subdivisions within method as applied to objects, namely, successive exhibition and connected aggregation. It may be recalled that priority and posteriority with respect to place or time is held to be fundamental to the first and irrelevant to the second. Bentham allows that the two forms may be found together in the same project of arrangement, but he considers the distinction itself to be sharp and irreducible. "Arrangement of the names of the objects in a determinate figure, such as a line vertical or horizontal, is arrangement on the principle of lineal succession; arrangement of them under a common denomination, is arrangement on the principle of aggregation and enclosure." From this graphic description one gets the impression that in successive exhibition the materials are laid out, exposed, or delineated seriatim, whereas in connected aggregation they are unified by means of an integrating device (a "common denomination") which obviates detailed exposure. Or perhaps it can be said that in the one form of methodization a process is exposed, while in the other a structure is defined.

It is hard to avoid the feeling that the two forms, though indeed quite distinguishable, are necessarily complementary. The question is not simply whether they happen to be found together; they cannot be found apart. And it cannot even be said that they are two forms of arrangement; they are two phases of any arrangement. Any successive exhibition of materials is (or becomes) a connected aggregation when considered as a whole. And going beyond Bentham's view of priority and posteriority, we may say that any connected aggregation is characterized by priority and posteriority, both (*a*) temporally, in so far as it comes into being, and (*b*) within its own order, when analyzed (*i*) with respect to what is more and what is less important, and (*ii*) with respect to what is dependent on what. Every methodic process requires subaltern integrating devices. As a terminated whole, it may be considered a grand or multifaceted product. Correspondingly, every connecting structure, being methodically arrived at, has a career, or represents some phase of a process; and, being analyzable, has gradations within it. This formulation may be stated in a manner which both emphasizes the interdependency of the two "forms" and preserves something of the spirit of Bentham's distinction: In so far as any arrangement involves arranging, priority and posteriority are present; in so far as any arranging culminates in arrangement, a connecting structure or "enclosure" is present.

Reformulation helps Bentham up to a certain point. His own conception of priority and posteriority is excessively narrow, applying exclusively to space and time, and overlooking logical, structural, or valuational criteria. His conceptions of succession and aggregation are almost comically irrelevant to the manifestations of method in science, philosophy, art, and everyday conduct. Beyond restatement, however, there are inherent limitations. Bentham's explanatory illustration of succession in terms of "fifty guineas disposed in a row," and of aggregation in terms of the same guineas enclosed in a box, betrays a general approach to method. He cannot really decide how literal or how figurative the illustration is. In his philosophic reckoning methodic activity always does seem to reduce to lining up or boxing in—that is, to applying schemes, correcting irregularities, revealing incongruities. In the last analysis, once again, it may be the concept of arrangement that perpetuates all of the difficulties; but this concept, after all, is central in Bentham.

Bentham's conception of method is best adapted to classificatory procedures. Not at all surprising is his statement: "It is by Natural History, in greater proportion, than by any other branch of art and science, that exercise is afforded for observation and for method." And yet this conclusion, in itself strange and even irresponsible, is out of accord with Bentham's conception of logic as properly concerned with the "entire field of human thought and action"; that is to say, not only with "the whole field of art and science" but with "the field of ordinary, i.e., unscientific thought, and ordinary, i.e., unartificial action, or say practice." Method being in Bentham's view virtually synonymous with logic, there can hardly be much sense in supposing it exemplified more fully by one field than another. In the light of the stated scope of logic and method, why is "methodization" confined to "objects" and "discourse"? Are all actions and all projects of art, for instance, to be subsumed under one or the other of these categories? Here we have a case of almost radical disparity between a philosophic program and its embodiment. So far as the theory of method is concerned, no dish provided by Bentham really lives up to his bill of fare.

In place of the somewhat oppressive Benthamite enterprise of maintaining rectitude, Bentham's own idea of invention suggests a more attractive approach to method. Invention, it will be recalled, presupposes imagination, which in turn presupposes abstraction. Imagination is combinatorial, compounding and placing the products of abstraction. With every detail of this one could argue at length, especially with the postulate that all invention ultimately requires abstraction. But it is rather the direction of the analysis, and its implications for method, that concerns us now. Invention is "imagination, taken under command by attention, and directed to the accomplishment of some particular object or end in view." Within this inventive process there are two main factors, one method, the other chance insight. Method is the opposite of chance. It is designed to keep the domain of imagination in order, so that amidst the data it has arranged, a new discovery may be recognized. Or, looking at the matter another way, the function of method is to provide order for whatever discoveries arise within the inventive process, and thereby to promote invention. Invention, free of regulatory restraints on imagination, is flexible. Method, after being itself bred by invention, introduces fixity. And this is what appears to be implied when Bentham calls it an instrument—"an instrument in the hands of invention, of discovery, and of observation." (We shall return to the notion of "instrument" in a later section.)

Conceding the inevitably pedestrian nature of much

that is entitled to be called methodic activity, one nevertheless craves a more determinately conceived relation between method and invention than the mere gesture of each to the other that Bentham permits. To say that method is itself a product of invention is not unsound. But it calls for qualification.

1. If invention is to be regarded as a purposive process, and not as totally spontaneous activity with novel effects, it would seem to be itself methodic. Method, in other words, would seem to be essential to invention as invention, and not just to be something that enters the scene as an auxiliary of invention after the latter has bred it. To say that a method is produced by invention would mean that it is the product of another method, an inventive method. There is nothing strange about this. It is no more strange than acquiring a perspective on the basis of a previous perspective. And in fact, the method that produces may belong to a perspective different from the perspective of the method it produces.

2. Though it is possible for a method to be produced by (methodic) invention, it is not necessary. (*a*) A method may be developed imperceptibly, and may emerge from a vast complex of institutional changes, individual needs, impulses, desires, and physical occurrences. In this sense, it may be no more than a "development," an effect of confluent events which, when understood, convey the impression of being uniquely determining historical antecedents. (*b*) When a method is not bred by invention in the sense of being a designed effect, it may yet be an indirect or remote effect of invention, with a liberal mixture of chance. The inventive origin may have been dispersed in the complex of

events. This strain (as distinguished from a project) of invention may have persisted over a long period of time through the vehicle of individual effort or the unconscious collaboration of various individuals. In none of these respects can it be said that the method was the product of a clear-cut purpose.

There are two points at which Bentham's inquiry indirectly opens the way to a fuller conception of the relation between method and invention. The first is in his repeated reference to "the art of methodization." The second is in his description of methodization as "the exercise of what may be termed the tactic faculty."

In analyzing what may be implied by "the art of methodization," it becomes convenient to devise a skeletal framework on which to fit possible divergencies of activity. Although this framework cannot support all of the basic factors that (as we shall subsequently see) enter into method, it is adequate to the immediate purpose at hand. Whoever is said to act methodically (1) chooses a mode of conduct (2) to be directed in a given way (3) to a particular set of circumstances (4) for the attainment of a result. These four simple factors required by the conjunction of "art" and "method" can each assume different forms. The mode of conduct adopted may consist in (1a) established practice, in (1b) established practice modified by idiosyncratic technique, or in (1c) essentially idiosyncratic, private practice. Whatever procedure is adopted, it may be utilized (2a) strictly and in accordance with prescription, or (2b) loosely, variably, and with a discretionary relation to prescription, or (2c) uniquely, in consequence of predominant reliance on insight. The circumstances under which the procedure is utilized may be (3a) definitely classifiable circumstances, or (3b) circumstances ranging from the expected and classified down to the minimal circumstances that would allow the procedure. And the result toward which the activity aims may be (4a) an envisaged or familiar type of result, or (4b) an indefinite result accepted as such in terms of desirability, or (4c) a relatively novel result. These forms are not exhaustive, but their possible combinations help to explain the differences that prevail when we speak variously of the art of surgery, the art of writing fiction, the art of management, the art of building, or the art of swimming.

Of immediate pertinence is the fact that every possible combination could plausibly exemplify an art of methodization, Bentham to the contrary notwithstanding. On the basis of both the letter and the spirit of his approach, Bentham would be least likely to accept as appropriate factors (2b), (2c), (4b), and (4c). Assuming the combination of (1a), (2a), (3a) or (3b), and (4a) to be acceptable to Bentham, the "art" of method would lie both in the degree of fidelity to the course chosen, including mastery of its details, and in the skill by which it is adapted to the circumstances, including attainment of the expected result. But if it is reasonable to accept what Bentham would not—and the multifariousness of the activities historically acknowledged as methodic and as art seems to favor this—we should be justified in regarding invention, with all of its chance insights, as sometimes an essential part of method.

Just as, in the conception of art, the relative emphasis

may be either on executive skill and perfection of practice or on inventive making, so analogously in the conception of a "tactic faculty" two strains of meaning may be educed. One of these has to do with a prepared order eligible for application to appropriate circumstances; the other has to do with a power of adjusting practice to variable circumstances. The one emphasizes a fund or store of techniques whose function is anticipatory; the other emphasizes resourceful practice precisely in the face of the unanticipated. An individual's "tactics," like an army's, may consist either of characteristic procedures for coping with what may come, or of ingenious decisions devised when necessary. Although strictly speaking these two manifestations of the tactical may coexist and even be complementary, they are profoundly different in the psychological and moral influence they tend to exert. The one seeks to minimize risk, to emphasize the repeatedly valuable, to turn effort away from innovation, speculation, and daring. The other emphasizes willingness to err in the cause of discovery, and the desirability of taking untried steps. The one points to the wastefulness of adventure and the need to regularize. The other points to the prospect of adventure, and its inevitability. It is the former of the two strains that Bentham identifies with method; it is the latter that would allow within method a role for inventiveness. In Bentham's eyes tactic is no doubt perfectly equivalent to arrangement, as its etymology from the Greek *taktikos* indicates. But tactic is a trait of extensive importance, for it is closely connected not merely with arrangement but with control. The methodic man achieves control either by what popular locution calls "know-how" or by the ability to make, to say, and to do under increasingly diversified conditions. Tactic implies a perspective of voluntary coping, through which method confronts the indifference or recalcitrancy of existence. The idea of "control" is most often associated with scientific method, and specifically with the technological power conferred by scientific knowledge. But tactical control is more fundamental. Common to all methods, it is the elemental discipline that precedes methodic consummations.

IV

We are ready now for a strikingly different approach. The term "method," says Coleridge, cannot, "otherwise than by abuse, be applied to a mere dead arrangement."[3] For we must note that *methodos* "literally means a way, or path, of transit." The notion of transition, movement, one step after another, is central. Though in all instances of method we do attempt to classify and arrange, above all we forge ahead. And even this is not enough. The passage, the movement, must have two further characteristics—"progress" and "unity." Any arrangement must contain within itself a "principle of progression." It must be a "progressive transition," and the "way" must exhibit "unity." Thus to Coleridge, Socrates' discussion with the slave in *Meno* and Euclid's *Elements* are instances of method, and they are commonly regarded as methodic for good reason. But the alphabetical order of a dictionary is not methodic. It is dead. It lacks what Coleridge calls "continuity," an attribute without which a transition cannot be progressive.

What is entailed by these requirements of unified, progressive arrangement and movement? What is the basic function of method? And what does the presence of method mean? Method comes into being, Coleridge believes, when certain conditions of the mind obtain. When the mind rouses itself from a state of exclusive passivity; when there ceases to be "an habitual submission of the understanding to mere events and images"; and when, in more positive terms, "the mind becomes accustomed to contemplate, not things only, but likewise *relations* of things, there is immediate need of some path or way of transit from one to the other of the things related;—there must be some law of agreement or contrast between them; there must be some mode of comparison; in short, there must be method. We may, therefore, assert that the *relations of things* form the prime objects, or, so to speak, the *materials* of method; and that the contemplation of those relations is the indispensable condition of thinking methodically." The last two words in this quotation are as important as any of the others. To Coleridge, method implies thinking. The reason that art, science, and philosophy are all methodic is that they are all ways of thinking—about relations of things; specifically, ways of discovering or attempting to discover what these relations are. Thus the purpose of method is always to arrive at truth.

Thinking about the relations of things presupposes the sensing or feeling of things. We cannot search for connections unless we are sensitive to, unless we absorb, the elements to be connected or united. Hence, "method must result from the due mean, or balance, between our passive impressions and the mind's reaction on them,"—"between the passive impression received from outward things, and the internal activity of the mind in reflecting and generalizing." The "events and images" which by themselves can arrest the mind in a pre-methodic lethargy are necessary as stimuli and food for method. There are two extremes that upset the balance of method. One is indiscriminate passion, the consequence of passivity. The other is excessive reflection and generalization. The former breeds "confusion"; the latter, "exuberance." Confusion is a symptom of "sterility," while exuberance is a symptom of "flying from the sense of reality." Mrs. Quickly in *Henry IV* illustrates the former trait; Hamlet, the latter. Hamlet's fault, as Coleridge sometimes puts it, is to "methodize to excess, ever philosophizing, and never descending to action." Strictly, in Coleridge's view, the former extreme is far more serious; for unlike this, it is not simply an interference with the forms of method, an obstacle to consummation, but is utterly inimical to method—destructive of the activity in which method consists, and inclined to be incorrigible.

Coleridge distinguishes two main kinds of relations among things, "the relation of law" and "the relation of theory." (The term "relation" functions ambiguously, sometimes appearing to signify what is imposed upon things, and sometimes what is discovered in them. This ambiguity also arises in the use of the term "law," though here Coleridge is aided by his ancillary doctrine that law as a rule laid down and law as a characteristic of being are ultimately one and the same. The details of Coleridge's metaphysics and theology do not concern us.) Through law we perceive what "must be"; through theory, what "is." Law implies mental certainty and ontological necessity, "necessary connection." Coleridge develops a fairly complicated scheme of the sciences:

some sciences, by their nature, are concerned with law; others, often by dint of historical retardation, are concerned with theory. (The term "hypothesis" in Coleridge represents yet a third and lower degree of discerning relations, presumably perceiving what "may" be, and suggesting either a conjecture or a conceptual fiction.) "The relations of law and theory have each their methods. Between these two, lies the method of the fine arts, a method in which certain great truths, composing what are usually called the laws of taste, necessarily predominate; but in which there are also other laws, dependent on the external objects of sight and sound, which these arts embrace." Though all methods aim at truth, method which is concerned with relations of law is most perfect and fundamental, for it fulfills supremely this underlying ideal. The "constructions of science and literature" alike derive their methodic excellence from "that just proportion, that union and interpenetration, of the universal and the particular."

Every methodic project rests on an "idea." The idea not only starts and propels the movement; it imparts direction, and therefore introduces progression into the pattern that is to be wrought. By virtue of the fact that it is a "key note" of "the harmony" to follow, it ensures unity, in the form of a principle by which things may be connected and united. Coleridge uses different terms to describe this initial force. Most often it is the "leading idea" or "guiding idea," the "leading thought" or "guiding thought." It is the "initiative" or "mental initiative." Depending on the context, it is variously called a "preconception," a "previous act and conception of the mind," a "master idea," a "prior purpose," a "pre-cogitation." Sometimes the idea is said to arise, not in clear and mandatory form, but as an "instinct," a "vague appetency" through which the idea "first announces its incipient germination." The leading idea is the impetus by which a method is launched: it is "some well-grounded purpose, some distinct impression of the probable results, some self-consistent anticipation." Declaring kinship with Francis Bacon, Coleridge says that "an idea is an experiment proposed, an experiment is an idea realized." When at one point he distinguishes "two main directions of human activity . . . trade and literature," and describes the methodic character of each, he emphasizes that "in both there must be a mental antecedent; but that in the one [trade] it may be an image or conception received through the senses, and originating from without . . . while in the other the initiative thought, the intellectual seed, must itself have its birth-place within, whatever excitement from without may be necessary for its germination."

In his principle of an "initiative of all method" Coleridge implicitly combines the notions of act, theme, and purpose. "Act" in particular implies more than what is traditionally called "mental operation." It implies that mind is not simply and primarily impelled to its discoveries by external objects or happy accidents. It would be better to say that mind avails itself aggressively of what there happens to be. Accidental discoveries there indeed are, but the reason they are discoveries and not merely accidents is that there has been "prior purpose" and "previous conception." "That which unites and makes many things *one* in the mind of man, must be an act of the mind itself, a manifestation of intellect, and not a spontaneous and uncertain production of circumstances." The emphasis on intellect, in turn, is more than an emphasis on the source of the initiative; it specifies the initiative as thought rather than feeling. Although Coleridge has insisted that method results from "the due mean or balance between our passive impressions and the mind's own reaction on the same," the present emphasis is on initiation, not reaction.

Sometimes, Coleridge concedes, "the predominance of some mighty passion takes the place of the guiding thought." His preference compromising with his candor, he describes the result as "the method of nature" rather than distinctively the method of man. The notion of a method of nature he finds too universally acknowledged to be taken lightly, and he attributes the source of the notion to "the religious instinct." Thus, "all method supposes a union of several things to a common end, either by disposition, as in the works of man; or by convergence, as in the operations and products of nature." Thought, then, initiates and guides what are properly the methods of man; passion reflects the underlying operation of nature. Thought in essence establishes connections; imagination and passion establish fusion, they are "co-adunative."

One might say that for Coleridge method is a compound of system and animation. It may be found in individual activity or in social trends—in a man's everyday conduct, in a developing science, in a poet's work, in the practices of a school. But routine individual conduct without a unifying principle of life and without a "purpose in view" is "mere orderliness without method"; and so is scientific practice that consists in classification regarded as self-sufficient rather than as a tool of explanation, law, and ever wider systematization. Nor is "a mere mode or set fashion of doing a thing" to be identified with method. Mere activity is no more methodic than mere arrangement. "The terms system, method, science, are mere improprieties of courtesy, when applied to a mass enlarging by endless appositions, but without a nerve that oscillates, or a pulse that throbs, in sign of growth or inward sympathy." Movement, then, as well as order, can be lifeless. Bentham's "end in view" is a condition of organization; Coleridge's "purpose in view" is an active force.

"All things, in us, and about us, are a Chaos, without method." This expresses Coleridge's conviction that method lies deep in the roots of human affairs. Thus, "from the cotter's hearth or the workshop of the artisan to the palace or the arsenal, the first merit . . . is, that everything be in its place. Where this charm is wanting, every other merit loses its name. . . . Of one, by whom it is eminently possessed, we say proverbially, he is like clock-work." But such regularity and pattern are methodic precisely because they are a means and not an end in themselves. With respect to time (as distinct from place), "the man of methodical industry and honorable pursuits . . . realizes its ideal divisions, and gives a character and individuality to its moments. If the idle are described as killing time, he may be justly said to call it into life and moral being, while he makes it the distinct object not only of the consciousness, but of the conscience." Coleridge finds no disparity between inspiration and life on the one hand, and habit on the other. He speaks frequently of the habit of method, or of the man of methodic habit. What counts is the content and function of the habit. There are habits of passivity and routine, but the habit of looking forward to a goal or of planning steps is essential to method. Shakespeare, for Coleridge, is the most splendid example of the marriage between inspiration and methodic habit, confounding those "who tread the enchanted ground of poetry [and who] do not even suspect that there is such a thing as method to guide their steps." In poetry, method "not only has a necessary existence, but the strictest philosophical application." Where, as in Shakespeare, "the habit of method is present and effective, things the most remote and diverse in time, place, and outward circumstance, are brought into mental contiguity and succession, the more striking as the less expected." This is the process of unification. Shakespeare, who violated the dramatic "unities" of time, place, and action, achieved a more fundamental unity by his sense of law, and specifically, by his disclosure of the laws of human feeling and conduct.

From the impulsion and foresight of the guiding idea there results always some structure. But the presence of structure must be understood broadly and carefully. Anywhere in ordinary speech or practice, though there be no formal project involved, there may be "method in the fragments." Coleridge regards Plato as the most methodic of all philosophers. In Plato, the "poetic philosopher," there are no conclusions set out in the manner ordinarily regarded as "systematic," any more than there are in Shakespeare, the "philosophic poet." Plato's method interconnects the facts and the data of the methodic process itself. Accordingly, "the *education* of the intellect, by awakening the *method* of self-development, was his proposed object, not any specific information that can be conveyed into it from without. He desired . . . to place [the mind] in such relations of circumstances as should gradually excite its vegetating and germinating powers to produce new fruits of thought, new conceptions, and imaginations, and ideas." What emerges with unity from Plato is the career of thought. Its possibilities and its pitfalls are the materials that are dealt with in determining the laws of intellectual life. "It is strange . . . that the writings of Plato should be accused of estranging the mind from sober experience and substantial matter of fact, and of debauching it by fiction and generalities;—Plato, whose method is inductive throughout, who argues on all subjects not only from, but in and by, inductions of facts; who warns us, indeed, against that usurpation of the senses, which quenching the *lumen siccum* of the mind, sends it astray after individual cases for their own sakes . . . but who so far oftener, and with such unmitigated hostility, pursues the assumptions, abstractions, generalities, and verbal legerdemain of the sophists!" Plato's work, then, embodies the process of method in its perfect form, achieving "that just proportion, that union and interpenetration, of the universal and the particular," as well as "that due mean between a passiveness under external impression, and an excessive activity of mere reflection."

In an almost parenthetical manner, both at the beginning and at the end of the section on method in *The*

Friend, Coleridge makes references to "the method of the will." The first reference suggests a distinction between method as relating to the will and method as relating to the understanding, the former apparently illustrated by "method in the duties of social life." And Coleridge states here that the burden of his own discussion will deal with the realm of the understanding. The second reference, however, is of a quite different kind, Coleridge contending that "all true reality has both its ground and its evidence in the will, without which as its complement science itself is but an elaborate game of shadows, begins in abstractions and ends in perplexity." Here he is speaking not of two realms within which method functions, but of the primacy of will in any instance of method whatever. "All speculative disquisitions must begin with postulates, which the conscience alone can at once authorize and substantiate: and from whichever point the reason may start, from the things which are seen to the one invisible, or from the idea of the absolute one to the things that are seen, it will find a chasm, which the moral being only, which the spirit and religion of man alone, can fill up."

V

It must be evident that the contrast between Bentham and Coleridge, whose theories of method were composed at about the same time, reflects in vivid form the kind of contrast in conceptual emphasis that has been held representative of the Enlightenment and Romanticism. Grouping and predictable structure as against movement and life; appeal to the tested and tried as against inspiration and novelty; love of uniformity as against excitement over "the pulse that throbs"; strategic remedy as against growth and uniqueness. The contrast is not one of formal incompatibility. The conceptual predilections of Bentham and Coleridge are grounded in metaphysical preferences, in selections of traits felt to be essential to understanding in the broadest terms. On the basis of this contrast taken by itself, one suspects that the difference between the two types of historical (or human) temper is more dependent, for the preservation of its meaning, on the difference between the individual theories, than the other way round. The imaginative energy of each theory is quite distinguishable from larger cultural forces, and the theories are highly intelligible in philosophic terms alone.

We are told, in Coleridge's extraordinary analysis,

that method requires "a principle of unity," "a union of several things to a common end," an act of mind which "unites and makes things one in the mind of man." We are not told whether this property of unity resides mainly in the plan, the process, or the product of method; or whether it must reside in all three. Nor are the contextual differences of the terms "unitary," "union," and "unification" explored. These desiderata would be less urgent if the idea of unity did not exercise such profound fascination for so many people.

If we say that a plan, a process, a product is (or worse, should be) characterized by unity, are we saying anything at all—anything, that is to say, other than that it is a plan, a process, a product? How can any complex be said to lack unity once it is named or identified? Metaphysically, those philosophers who have declared unity to be the most comprehensive genus, or the "simplest" of all ideas, whatever the difficulties besetting them, are in a sense wiser than Coleridge and many another for whom the presence or absence of unity in things human is a critical problem. For unity is always in some sense predicable of whatever can be said to be discriminated, whether it be an aggregate, a "buzzing confusion," or an unexplored subject-matter.

What, then, must be meant by the frequent contention that a theory or a work of art "lacks unity," or by the commendatory attribution of unity to a product? There is most certainly a property that is present or legitimately sought in such cases: not unity, but some specific kind of unity. A theory that is said to violate the requirement of "unity" is unitary enough to be that theory and no other; but it may be, for example, sym-

bolically redundant, conceptually redundant, or defi-
cient in explanatory linkage of data. A play that is
said to "lack unity" is one and the same play—having
enough "unity" not to be confused by its detractors with
any other—but it may be diffuse by the standards that
happen to prevail, or unintelligible to audiences in the
sequence of its official "parts." In these and all analogous cases an expectation is unfulfilled. An implicit de-
mand is frustrated or left intact. Redundancy, novel
relations among components, absence of recognizable
sequences, all violate types of unity that have served as
means of assimilation. They exceed the limits of an established tolerance. They leave habits of total grasp
inapplicable, and they threaten the standard by which
a structure is recognized. In subsequent historical estimation, of course, any such deviation from the type of
unity that is expected may be for better or worse. The
deviant type of unity, or a changed criterion of unity,
may come to be accepted. And the value of the new
criterion will depend on what general advantages are
yielded by the perspective which harbors and deter-
mines it.

Seeing in method a basic trait of man, Coleridge is
eager to detect its teleological nature. "Unity" for him
implies intensity and dedication, perfection of en-
deavor. It rescues method from groping. For to Coleridge method and groping are no more compatible than
they are to Bentham, different as the reasons may be.
The guiding idea, guarantor of unity, dominates the
material and fixes the purview of relevancy. In sublime
singleness of purpose, it paves the way toward consummation. What Coleridge plainly admires is the type of

unity that lies in the steady role which an anticipative quality of mind plays throughout the methodic process. Unfortunately, he fails to distinguish the different respects in which this role realizes itself. He overlooks the fact that unity of vision and intent does not necessarily entail the same kind of unity in the result, nor even in the transition from vision to result. Strictly speaking, none of these three phases of unity implies either of the others, despite Coleridge's faith in the propagative and telic efficacy of the first. Integrity of vision, the persistence of an aim, is not by itself executive. The ensuing activity, in spite of its uniform continuation as activity, may be divisive in various ways. Over and above such divisions, to be sure, it may possess a subtler type of unity than the homogeneous forwardness customarily sought in it—it may possess a unity of eventual function, wherein the different ingredients, some of them seemingly alien and incidental, nevertheless promote the result. This transitional activity might be called "unification," in so far as it consists in the ultimate organization of disparate complexes. The unification of complexes, we may then say, is to be distinguished from, though it may be abetted by, "unitary" (unswerving) vision. The result of the process could be called a "union" of complexes, if a separate name were desired for the terminal phase, and if it were realized that a particular kind of unification might result in more than one kind of union.

Does a methodic process necessarily "unify"? Qualifications are still wanting. A method may terminate in physical separations or in conceptual distinctions, thereby achieving pluralization. On the other hand, these separations and distinctions may be made possible only because the various strands of a *problem,* its ingredient aspects, have been brought together. The strands of a problem too are natural complexes. In certain methods of teaching, which proceed by proliferating issues and multiplying options, the student may emerge with a large number of indecisive ideas. But it can be argued that precisely this type of process intensifies and interrelates the resources of the student. "Unification" is to be regarded as inevitable, then, only in the sense that, whether method terminates in a bringing together or a separating out, methodic order as such has a unifying effect. A unifying effect may be good or it may be bad: there is methodic unification in philosophic understanding and methodic unification in imperial conquest. In pointing to Plato as an exemplar of method, Coleridge clearly recognizes the difference between the unifying effect of a persistent procedure and unification in the sense of fusion or combination, as well as the greater importance of the former. The Platonic dialogues most often culminate suspensively, but their unitary function is to be found in the inviolate spirit of their attack.

What does it mean to say, and what reason is there to believe: 1) that in method there is a guiding idea rather than several guiding ideas; 2) that guiding ideas *initiate* a methodic enterprise; and 3) that the guiding factors in method are always "ideas" or "thoughts"?

1*a.* The social conditions of human production, and the individual trends of thought adapted to them, make it difficult to imagine a methodic undertaking which does not rest on *a* plan. We do engage in numerous activities emanating from uncertain intent. The activities themselves are very easily describable without our having to formulate any simple or single aim at all. There is a tendency, however, to regard such activities as non-methodic. We assume that we are "confused" when our course of conduct reflects no unitary impetus or resolve. We explain our conduct as habitual or mechanical, and we describe the underlying ideas as indeterminate. Method after all, we say, is purposive. But this begs the very question. There is no reason why activity may not be purposive without resting on a *single* purpose. Shakespeare, Bach, and Plato do not acquire their intelligibility from our knowledge of an explicitly stated purpose or any one dominant purpose. Nor is it likely that any explicit single purpose actually underlay each of their products. Yet if any human works are to be regarded as methodic, theirs must be. Coleridge's bias in favor of the "philosophic" character of method warrants the observation that a philosophic product certainly need not reflect a unique aim, a "master idea." If the major categories of a system were ever reduced to a single category, the result would be of dubious value. The tendency to look for the one key, the clue, to a methodic product is enchanting but treacherous. The philosopher and the artist, much more than the scientist, have reason to distrust the search for a decisive basis of their work; in philosophy and art the meanings derived from the product are more heavily dependent upon the experiential range and collaborative power of the interpreting community.

1*b*. But in the discipline of science, the notion of one guiding idea for each project is equally questionable.

In any instance of scientific activity, there are to be found procedures common to all instances of scientific method, and variant procedures which, though harmonious with the common, are extensions or innovations dictated both by the particular situation or problem at hand and by the particular science concerned with it. The common or general procedures of scientific method are not guided by any idea peculiar to the given instance of activity; the ideas that guide them (for example, principles of consistency or principles of evidence) have been established beforehand and may be no more important in this than in any other instance. The variant procedures in the given instance may be guided by ideas characteristic of the particular science or by ideas germane to the specific conditions of the problem, or by both kinds of ideas. That all these procedures should be called into play by one basic idea is plausible; but the one basic idea alone cannot guide them.

2a. The guiding thought, for Coleridge, is an "initiative." But there are two senses in which a methodic process can be initiated. An idea may (i) initiate a process in the sense that it prompts, stimulates, or arouses it. Or, an idea may (ii) initiate a process in the sense that it serves as an essential first step. The writing of a novel may be initiated in sense (i) by an idea that prolonged idleness is bad for novelists, and in sense (ii) by an idea of the relation between sexuality and love. The idea about what novelists should do functions as a circumstantial initiative; the idea about love, as a thematic initiative. In the first sense the idea is temporally and efficiently prior; in the second, it is substantively prior, and it functions as a required basis. (To describe these senses in terms of "causal" and "logical" priority, respectively, raises difficulties. For in the first, the idea may serve as a fortuitous, unique, and merely sufficient condition of methodic activity; so that the full requirement for "causal connection" is not realized. And in the second, the idea may be essential without standing in "logical" relation to what follows it: to reduce artistic or moral sequences to "logical" sequences is, to say the least, a debatable undertaking.)

2b. Take the common procedures that are repeated in every instance of a method. The ideas that guide them do not initiate them but are coeval with them. In terms of awareness by individuals either the procedures or the ideas may come first. The guiding function occurs not once and for all but continuously. And the idea that guides is here analogous not to a spark that ignites but to a hand that limits and bounds movement. To point the direction is not necessarily to lead the way, and to lead the way is not necessarily to have initiated the project, or to anticipate its result. Coleridge, overlooking distinctions of this kind, is most interested in the unique procedures of each project, and in the anticipated result. His "initiative" idea anticipates and generates and guides the whole of a methodic enterprise, its wholeness. Historically, the vast diversity of methodic processes in human life reveals much greater latitude than Coleridge recognizes. Plans may either precede methodic activity entirely or emerge articulately in the course of it; a structure may be either totally envisioned beforehand or fall into place gradually as though its parts were independently animate and mutually harmonious. Coleridge's "idea," which both initiates and guides, is most plausibly applicable to the adumbration of specific problem solutions in science. It is conceptual foresight, which helps to shrink the otherwise overwhelming number of obstacles to inquiry. That mathematics and natural science, incontrovertibly progressive, should bewitch Coleridge, is no accident. Considering the traits that attract him, it is always a fair question whether he is legislating the nature of method or consenting to discover it.

When Coleridge speaks of guiding ideas he is expressing a passion for new ideas. And he sees new ideas as methodologically fundamental because in his outlook method and invention are one. When only the inventive forms of method fully deserve the name, method becomes a eulogistic concept. Each instance of its employment becomes a penetration by man of natural complexes that would otherwise be inaccessible. Hence every idea is "an experiment proposed"—a new experiment; and every experiment is "an idea realized"—a guide vindicated. This opposite extreme from Bentham is equally narrow, its aristocratic air neglecting the existence of the prosaic and everyday methods. Bentham's insistent differentiation of method and invention has its advantages. It permits us when necessary to distinguish, as Coleridge can not, between general or repeatable procedures on the one hand and the methodic accomplishment of uniqueness on the other. Its own disadvantages, as we have seen, lie in its tendency to see method solely in the dimension of ramified technique. For Bentham method means salubrious economy, the repudiation of superfluity and waste; for

Coleridge it means vision and vital development. Arrangement and economy are accepted by Coleridge, but as dramatic, mobile feats of self-discipline in the approximation to law. Vision, for Bentham, is not anticipation of the end but perception of the means. Nothing, for him, so distracting as "the nerve that oscillates . . . the pulse that throbs."

3a. Do mathematical methods, choreographic methods, mining methods, methods of playing second base, military methods, manufacturing methods, and all other methods rest on "ideas" (or "thoughts")? If resting on ideas is taken to mean that methodic activity is necessarily purposive, the answer would have to be, yes. Method cannot be either purely mechanical or purely fortuitous. But if it is taken to mean that method necessarily requires intellection in the sense of propositional utterance, the answer would ultimately have to be, no. Coleridge describes the leading idea as "an act of the mind itself, a manifestation of intellect, and not a spontaneous and uncertain product of circumstances." This identification of guiding idea with "preconception," "pre-cogitation," "previous act and conception of the mind" is not merely an emphasis on intellect but a symptom of the kind of intellectualism that has permeated the major traditions of philosophy, including the views of those who are enemies of "intellect" in the sense of "rationality," and of those whose approach would ordinarily be thought wholly at odds with that of Coleridge. Coleridge contends that method aims or ought to aim at the discovery of "laws," of "truths," of what "must be." On this assumption, science, aiming at valid propositions, would be the purest example of method. The musician and the painter, the fencer and the chess player, the mason and the carpenter, the theologian and the philosopher, the student and the teacher, if held to be methodic, would in effect be scientists in their respective media, all moving, grandly or modestly, toward the disclosure of law. But there are limits even to the most ingenious of reductive interpretations. To think of "trade" as methodically seeking truth is down-right funny.

Now purposive activity does not necessarily imply quest for veridical conclusions. Veridical conclusions are termini of inference, and certain types of sequence in methodic activity are not inferential at all. In fact, for an indefinitely large number of methods, inference plays only a minor, subordinate role. The products of these methods are "conclusions" only in a temporal and positional respect; they are endings without the status of "truths." Under certain conditions they are com-pelled to be what they are and where they are. But they are not compelled by evidence or testimony. They may show us something; or they may accomplish something for us; they need not defend, argue, or tell us anything. If veridical conclusions are thus foreign to the nature of some types of methodic pursuit, so are veridical ex-pectations. Purposive activity merely as such may con-sist not only or not at all in formulated anticipation but in desires, inclinations, feelings, needs, or urges that aim at making or doing, and that persist until such an aim for well or ill is consummated.

3b. The idea as "an experiment proposed" can be broadened in meaning beyond Coleridge's own pro-pensity to understand it as the proposed test of a suspected truth. To be faithful to all manifestations of method, the experiment proposed would be an "experience proposed," a direction begun. Then mountain-climbing and sculpture would not have to be propositionalized. They would be human utterances awaiting completion, quite on an equal status with assertions awaiting support. The "proposal" in all cases of method would be the voluntary selection of a complex for manipulation. And in this sense it would be inevitable.

It is time to explore other Coleridgian categories. How are "continuity" and "progress" to be recognized in human activity? These two traits alone would not seem to make activity methodic. A man who slips into the sea, who then struggles to remain alive and emerges from the water, can fairly be said to be engaged in activity that is continuous and progressive. Each movement or maneuver is in some sense connected with its predecessors and successors, and the totality of movements attains a result. The fact that the result is a consummation, that it is successful and desirable, even seems to "unify" what has happened. The activity is also purposive, despite the fact that it was not purposively initiated. Basically we could not say that the situation as a whole illustrated a method, but we could say that in the course of the situation various methodic processes were brought into play.

But assuming that a given case of human activity is methodic, in what sense is it therefore "continuous" and "progressive"? In what sense does *Meno* exemplify continuity and a common dictionary lack it? These specimens, chosen by Coleridge, are products of method rather than instances of methodization. If *Meno* has continuity, does anything follow about Plato's way of producing it? If a dictionary lacks continuity, does it follow that the ways of compiling it are discontinuous? In a strictly psychological and physical sense, transitional activity is almost unavoidably discontinuous: deliberative production gets interrupted—by sleep, by arbitrary cessation, by distraction. Just what does remain continuous in the production? One possible way of going about an answer is to examine the product with a view toward retrospectively inferring the attributes of the process. But when all is said and done, the whole question of continuity in the process seems curiously unimportant, probably because it is so hazy a question. The conceivable modes of continuous activity, the perspectives in which they are initiated, the criteria by which they are measured, are so numerous that the problem itself threatens to lapse into a tiresome exercise.

Turning, then, as Coleridge does, to the products themselves, both *Meno* and the dictionary are governed in their order by a principle of sequence among the parts. The alphabetical order of words, we should want to say, is a less complicated and more easily discernible order than that of *Meno;* in *Meno,* we should also want to say, there are actually several principles of sequence. Within each product every part is connected with some other, by virtue of the original purpose or plan of organization, with its philosophic or semantic or positional requirements. In this sense there is continuity in each. Is the one type of continuity a "more perfect" type of continuity than the other? In terms of a chosen standard of perfection we would be at liberty to say so. But which of innumerable standards would we dare claim to be mandatory? From each structure it would be possible to remove some part, say a given word, without impairing the relative "density" of the sequence or the continuity as such. From each structure certain other removals would destroy the sequence as originally construed. It is necessary, therefore, to conclude, not that the one product of method is continuous and the other discontinuous, or that the one is "more" continuous than the other, but that the one is perhaps more admirable than the other in the affairs of man. There may be every reason to say this, but it has nothing to do with the nature of method.

Must the analysis be the same with respect to the trait of "progression"? In both *Meno* and the dictionary there are plan, activity, and result. Each result has an actual beginning, middle, and ending which, if reversed, conflict with established expectations. Each exhibits a different kind of progression, a different "principle." Is one kind more perfect than the other, and of a perfection essential to method? It might be argued (in behalf of Coleridge) that in *Meno* the nature or meaning of each significant part is dependent on the progression as a whole, whereas in the dictionary each part is external to and independent of the progression. Thus a definition given in *Meno* requires the total context, whereas a definition in the dictionary does not. But might it not be counter-argued that if the dictionary definition is truly completed only when in turn we define its *components,* eventually all of the definitions and the whole of the dictionary would be required? Yes, they would be required, but not in the sequence by which the dictionary unfolds (progresses) as a dictionary. In *Meno* the ideas depend upon the context as it unfolds; in the dictionary, they depend upon other parts regardless of where they are located alphabetically or how they appear in the sequence of the whole. But—counter-arguing again—the definitions in *Meno* are not totally dependent upon the entire unfolding or progression of the dialogue. They are in part dependent upon meanings in the Greek language established before the composition of the dialogue, and in part dependent upon properties of language as such. Thus preexisting language and customary verbal interpretation constitute a perspective in which *Meno* as a whole is itself located. And on the other side of the matter, the definitions in the dictionary are not totally independent of the alphabetical sequence. For all verbal interpretation requires a manipulative economy of some kind. If it were not the device of the alphabet, it would have to be some other kind of order the unfolding of which would make available the fund of conventionally accumulated signs. To Coleridge, the dictionary lacks the kind of necessity in its unfolding that *Meno* has. The latter does plainly exhibit, moreover, a succession of interest stages which is as essential to the whole as the whole is to each stage. The kind of progression present in *Meno,* Euclid's *Elements,* and *Hamlet,* Coleridge tacitly identifies with all progression; and perhaps ultimately it is in this kind of concretely realized progression that his attribute of "unity" consists.

The pertinent issue now is not whether the dictionary exhibits progression, for it does, but whether its mode of progression is representative of a methodic product. The decision cannot be separated from an examination of other products and practices commonly acknowledged as methodic. Consider a finished product of sculpture. If there is any sequence or unfolding of component "parts" within this, it is certainly very different in kind from that of a novel, a symphony, a philosophic study, or a scientific theory. If there is "progression" of some kind, like that of the contours which extend from the lower to the higher areas, or from the higher to the lower, or from one side to another, it is not progression in Coleridge's sense: traits like beginning, middle, and ending are absent, as are "stages" and "conclusions." Sculpture and painting, be it noted, are as resistant to Bentham's conception of method as to Coleridge's. Their products do not exemplify "discourse"; nor, when they take any other form than groups or murals, do these products exemplify a "successive exhibition" or "connected aggregation" of "objects." To explain them, in Bentham's scheme, as products of invention rather than of method is to evade the issue, since method is still present as an "instrument" of invention.

The forms of progression not only vary but show a wide range of differences with respect to the presence or absence of stages, the nature of such stages as there are, the relative dependence of significant parts on the total sequence, or the scope, rigidity, and relevance of prior rules. A poem, a game of chess, a lecture, a masonry wall, a judicial decision, a psychiatric technique, an agricultural operation, a mathematical proof, and a financial transaction differ so conspicuously in the nature of the progression they involve, that the idea of progression must be understood far more broadly than Coleridge understands it, even when its importance is granted. For example, the notion of beginning, middle, and ending names factors that are less definite in a financial transaction than in a game of chess. Prior rules are less important for a poem than for a stone wall, though more important for a sonnet than for an epic. The spatial progression in the span of a bridge, the temporal progression in an agricultural operation, and the possibly non-spatial, non-temporal progression in a mathematical proof are in some way analogous to one another. But the principles of similarity present difficulties in the way of formulation that are undreamt of by Coleridge. And it is no simple problem to say how all these forms of methodic progression differ from non-methodic forms of progression, or from forms of progression in natural processes that are independent of man.

What is to be understood by the "due mean or balance" between "our passive impressions" (or "a passiveness under external impression") and "the mind's own reaction on the same" (or "an excessive activity of mere reflection")—the mean that Coleridge declares to be most basically constitutive of method? We may observe, first of all, that if method consisted in a mean, very little sense would be left in Coleridge's phrase "methodize to excess," by which he describes the reflective isolation of Hamlet and comparable postures that allegedly lose sight of the real world. This phrase, in contrast to "the mean," tacitly identifies method with reflection, and then assumes that there is another factor in life by which method must be tempered. The two usages are strangely incongruous: method as reflection can be

increased to excess; method as the mean between reflection and passive impression cannot, by definition,
be increased to excess, but only modulated to a more
perfect form. There is not much value in trying to
reconcile the different senses. We shall focus attention
on the "mean" usage, merely in deference to the greater
frequency of its occurrence. More important is the consideration that both usages are philosophically unsatisfactory. It is worth citing one test case for both. Mathematics is as close to "mere reflection" as anything can
be. Yet in our right mind we should scarcely regard
mathematical reasoning and mathematical invention as
an illustration of "methodizing to excess." Nor can we
regard pure mathematics as a mean between "passive
impression" and reflection. The "external impressions"
that Coleridge is thinking of are irrelevant in mathematical methods. The result is an irony; for Coleridge,
like almost everyone else, sees mathematics as par excellence the impressive manifestation of method.

The concept of a mean or balance carries with it an
initial persuasiveness and presumption of correctness,
however unexciting it may be for the speculative and
moral imagination. Common as well as philosophic
discourse links method and balance, each of which is
felt to be better than its opposite. Each seems unquali-
fiedly deserving of approbation. And the apparent rea-
sonableness of the association obscures the pertinent
questions. Does method imply any kind of balance?
Does balance imply any kind of method? Coleridge is
actually far more discriminating. He specifies one kind
of balance by selecting the extremes between which it
obtains. The categories of impression and reflection,

the one "passive," the other "active," mirror the dominant orientation of modern philosophy. Sometimes going by the names of sensation and intellection, or perception and conception, or the given and the constructed, they presuppose the same metaphysics with its inevitable direction of analysis. What Coleridge calls "method" others call "knowledge." Coleridge himself more or less implicitly emphasizes a close relation between method and knowledge, knowledge and "law" being two faces of the same ideal.

How is it to be determined whether and when there is a mean between impression and reflection? Grant that Mrs. Quickly represents one extreme and Hamlet the other, and that Plato, Shakespeare, and modern science represent a balance. Can these illustrations, so intimately joined to the framing of the conception, equip us to distinguish any methodic from any non-methodic practitioner? What about Protagoras, Anselm, Descartes, Hume, and Hegel—men who represent historical extremes of philosophic thought? Do they all violate the "due mean"? That these philosophers without exception are methodic is the necessary point of departure, whatever the consequences may be for the concept of a mean, or for the particular mean of which Coleridge is enamored, or for the possibility of ascertaining this mean. And what shall we say of Pericles, Innocent III, Napoleon, Disraeli, and Stalin? If these men are conceded to be methodic, did any kind of mean prevail in their action, or Coleridge's in particular? And by what standard would we recognize its presence? Do Dionysian and Apollonian tendencies in art represent one and the same mean of method? Do Racine, Wycherley, Strindberg, Tolstoy, Emily Dickinson, and T. S. Eliot? Do Giotto, Delacroix, and Matisse? And how relevant are the categories of impression and reflection, with or without a mean between them, to the methods of musical composition? The due mean must also be applied (with as little condescension as possible) to the methods of the butcher and the plumber, which are without sublimity but which qualify impressively in all other respects.

Does the mean come about by good luck, or is it achieved by a kind of pre-methodic method? Or is it the inherent quality of a certain type of "mind"? The extremes for Coleridge's mean are poorly formulated, if not unhappily chosen. If "passiveness under external impression" implies that certain traits of existence impose themselves and are not produced, then all men are passive in the same degree, and the methodic man would differ from the non-methodic man only in his attainment of the appropriate degree of reflection. Coleridge's methodic man, faced with one extreme which is constant, or in itself always an extreme, must modify the opposite extreme, which is in his control, until a certain state or relation is reached, however the arrival at this state may be determined. But if the mean is to be termed a "just proportion," it would seem that manipulation of both extremes is called for. And then the extremes would have to be re-defined. We would mediate, not between luck on the one side and reflection on the other, but between two extremes of activity, for example observational activity and reflective activity. Not that luck is ever wholly absent from method: both the conditions under which we would be said to mediate and the results of the mediation are subject to it, though we try to free ourselves from it by prognosis of the possible outcome.

But "observational activity" and "reflective activity" still do not comprise a pair that fits all the cases. Architects, mathematicians, manual laborers, politicians, musicians, and innumerable others remain elusive. And it seems unlikely that any pair of categories can be devised to fit Coleridge's bill. Imaginative pursuit of the best formulation must, therefore, cope with the stubborn suspicion that the very concept of the methodic mean is misleading. Although every methodic process presupposes data which are not of its own making and upon which operations are performed, a "balance," if this is what it must be called, can only be determined at the end and not at the beginning. But worse yet, the presence of a mean or balance can mean nothing more than that a method does get consummated. In whatever way a method eventuates, if it eventuates at all, it can always be described as a reconciliation ("mean" or "balance") between the basic factors involved—whatever these factors happen to be. A mean for method is not a prescription but an outcome. How are the proportions between the factors to be measured? They can be measured and defined only when a method issues in a product, something made, said, or done. As for a "due" mean, a "just" proportion, it is doubtful whether such a notion can be made significant by reference either to the beginning or to the end. The individual who aims to arrive at a methodically "just" result has only the experience of his predecessors to guide him. Had they too sought this justice, they would never have innovated in their methodic practice. He, of course, will innovate as they did, lest his mythical search for the methodically just extinguish such chance as he may have for attaining the humanly good.

Coleridge's "method of the will" brings to mind those philosophic outlooks which, feeling that something has been omitted from the mainstream of their inquiry, toss a final bouquet in the direction of will and conscience, like politicians who end their speeches with God. Is Coleridge's reference to will an extrinsic addendum, or is it a position which takes the methodic function of will seriously, as the position of William James, for example, does? It is hard to say. Coleridge, we suggested earlier, gives the impression of vacillating between the view that the method of the will represents a distinct methodic realm, which sometimes "passeth all understanding," and the view that this method is presupposed or embedded in all understanding. If we take the latter idea as the more interesting, it is possible to offer a variation. Method depends upon "will" in the sense that it requires the selection of something that concerns us, something that is relevant to our purposes. And method depends upon "conscience" in the sense that it requires the estimation of what concerns or is relevant to us. Selection and estimation are very closely related; strictly, they are inseparable. They are insistently present on an earthy and even subterranean level no less than as intellectual operations. They represent the human organism adopting a position from moment to moment and from situation to situation. They represent the individual perpetually judging his world. Method is primordial judgment become cohesive, deliberate, and qualified within a specific perspective. The judicative "conscience" also functions on a more explicit and refined level: over and above the rudimentary process of estimation, it rules on the planning, execution, and fruition of method. But it is concerned with the mundane and recurrent complexes that enter into method fully as much as with "chasms" and mysteries, and it is concerned with the province of action fully as much as with "speculative disquisitions."

VI

If, allowing for some simplification and some overlapping, we were to describe Bentham's conception of method as combinatorial and corrective, and Coleridge's as propulsive and vitalistic, we might describe Descartes's as prescriptive. Descartes's analyses are lacking in breadth of application. His *Discourse* is not about the nature of method but about the values and forms of one method in particular, "the method of rightly conducting the reason and seeking for truth in the sciences." That the quest for truth and the right conduct of reason imply exactly the same thing is assumed without question. In the earlier *Rules for the Direction of the Mind,* however, there are occasional generalizing divagations which are of considerable interest.[4] "By a method," says Descartes in elaborating Rule IV, "I mean certain and simple rules, such that, if a man observe them accurately, he shall never assume what is false as true, and will never spend his mental efforts to no purpose, but will always gradually increase his knowledge and so arrive at a true understanding of all that does not surpass his powers." Under Rule V he goes on to state that "method (*methodus*) consists entirely in the order and disposition of the objects towards which our mental vision must be directed if we would find out any truth. We shall comply with it exactly if we reduce involved and obscure propositions step by step to those that are simpler, and then starting with the intuitive apprehension of all those that are absolutely simple, attempt to ascend to the knowledge of all other by precisely similar steps."

Descartes identifies intuition and deduction as routes, paths, or ways (*viae*) of apprehending and certifying. These ways are, of course, purposive and directed. Whether they are in themselves specific methods—the two which most perfectly exemplify "method"—or merely operations presupposed by all method is far from clear. As ways of "knowing" they are declared to be exhaustive, and under Rule IV the warning is given that "the mind should admit no others." Under Rule VI, "the chief secret of method" is disclosed, namely, "that all facts can be arranged in a certain series, not indeed in the sense of being referred to some ontological genus such as the categories employed by philosophers in their classification, but in so far as certain truths can be known from others."

Men acquire method, Descartes says, by acquiring first of all a sense of order. And they can learn to acquire a sense of order by examining human disciplines that have already been developed and systematized in the highest possible degree—disciplines "in which order most prevails." These are illustrated and described under Rule X. "Such are the arts of the craftsmen who weave webs and tapestry, or of women who embroider or use in the same work threads with infinite modification of texture. With these are ranked all play with

numbers and everything that belongs to arithmetic.
. . . Since nothing in these arts remains hidden, and
they are wholly adjusted to the capacity of human cog-
nition, they reveal to us with the greatest distinctness
innumerable orderly systems, all different from each
other, but none the less conforming to rule, in the
proper observance of which systems of order consists
the whole of human sagacity."

In the Cartesian emphasis, rule is designed to lead
one ahead, not by pushing or propelling but by making
sharp, trustworthy illumination possible. A rule both
points and defines, and faithful observance of the rule
is virtually equivalent to completion of the project. The
"leading idea" of Coleridge supplies impetus and stimulus, and is most fully exemplified where "inspiration"
is present. But the Cartesian rule is designed precisely
to obviate dependency on inspiration, or more generally, dependency on contingent stimuli and indeterminate devices. The way ahead is to be prescribed by formulae, reason being in a sense the capacity to provide
such formulae. The rule is thus not merely a launching
or a promising beginning; it is not merely the way but
the whole way. It ensures economy; for diffuseness, regardless of the success it may permit, generates distraction and confusion, and courts irrelevancy, which is the
basis of imperfection. The rule represents purity of
vision, or exposure of all the simple elements in a compound.

Rule, we begin to perceive, is the basic antidote to
randomness in human affairs. And since presumably
the most reliable kind of antidote is the kind that leaves
least to individual discretion, the methodic process is

one of complete mechanization once the initial application is under way. To get properly started is to get properly finished. Mathematical analysis and embroidery, when discerned as appropriate to the complex at hand, leave no indeterminateness in the sequel. Although purely regularized activity is often regarded as the very reverse of methodic activity, the Cartesian context makes it plain that the particular form of heuristic regularization humanly chosen, and the auspices under which it is introduced, make the difference. The excitement and partial uncertainty of freely moving procedure is sacrificed to the majesty of pure reason.

For Descartes as for Coleridge, "method" tends to be a name for something good. And both tend to underplay any distinction between method and invention. Yet for Descartes the impersonal nature of method is in strong contrast to the kind of purposiveness that Coleridge idealizes. Coleridge thinks of human producers; Descartes, of productive disciplines. Any particular display of intentional activity that proceeds cohesively is methodic for Coleridge; whereas for Descartes a method is necessarily both repeatable and universally utilizable. Coleridge can speak of Plato's or Shakespeare's method; Descartes could speak only of the philosopher's or poet's method.

On the other hand, Descartes sees that the ultimate value of any activity regarded as a method depends on the possible diversity of its products no less than on their multiplicity. Method can produce *"innumerable orderly systems, all different from each other, but none the less* conforming to rule." In effect he removes himself from an exclusively industrial conception of method, which aspires to the achievement of "innumerable" products that are as uniform as possible. It is the distinction between craftsmanship and efficiency, both relying on universal processes for the attainment of results, but the one demonstrating its powers by variety, the other by quantity and similarity. The Cartesian rule is aimed at as many different circumstances as possible. The industrial rule aims to minimize the differences in the circumstances under which it is utilized. Method for Descartes seeks primarily to conquer unfavorable circumstances. Industrial method seeks primarily to exploit favorable circumstances.

Do all methods rest on rule? Is it desirable to speak of a method where there is no reason to believe that a rule is being applied? The answers are affected by the way in which the concept of rule is interpreted. If, instead of speaking of rule or law, we speak variously of policy, or guiding principle, or criterion of procedure, we are likely to give differing answers. So far as the Cartesian conception of rule is concerned, it is most pertinent, as Descartes indeed assumed, to the methods of pure mathematicians and of highly traditionalized artisans. But it clearly does not seem pertinent to other methods, methods which neither apply rules in actual practice nor aspire to rest on rules ideally. A theoretical biologist, an educational administrator, and a mile runner may or may not apply rules in the Cartesian manner. To the extent that they proceed without doing so they are not ordinarily deemed to be non-methodic. A poet or novelist can practice his art methodically in entire independence of such rules. To be sure, no activity can be wholly free of regulatory conditions in some sense if it is to be generically recognizable. There are restraining limits within which we study living bodies, or relate to persons, or run, or use language. But implicitly demarcating "rules" of this kind (limitations or boundaries) apply not only to methodic but to non-methodic pursuits, so that they can hardly be of distinctive importance.

A carpenter who ignores or violates a rule of construction in the interests of a particular situation is often regarded not as "less" but as "more" methodic. There are two good reasons for this. The first is that in certain perspectives of method the factor of general purposiveness outweighs the factor of regularity or propriety. In all method we want to be able to discern an order of some kind. But sometimes we are willing to abandon familiar patterns of reliability and predictability for a promise of greater reliability and wider predictability. We sense or we tacitly assume the frailty of tested procedures. Even when the innovation fails, the trait of being methodic is not jeopardized, for it becomes evident that the present availability of a method is subordinate in importance to the elevation of the methodic level.

The second reason is that to abandon a rule implies, not necessarily falling prey to chance, which might truly threaten the being of method, but greater reliance on discretion. From ancient times there have always been those who think of discretion as ideally replaceable by rule and who associate unregulated decision with the specter of chaos. But the very observance of rule, whether mathematical or administrative, requires discretion in its application; for a rule is designed to apply only under restricted conditions, and the conditions must be properly identified. And the abandonment of a rule need not imply a lapse into "disorder"; it may signify only the modification of a specific form of order.

What does it mean to say that in certain disciplines "nothing remains hidden"? Weavers, embroiderers, and arithmeticians, Descartes believes, practice such disciplines. They illustrate method in a form that is very simple but at the same time paradigmatic. The ideal presumably is for all disciplines ultimately to contain nothing hidden. Now Descartes has told us that method permits innumerable different applications. Uniqueness is therefore present in each of these applications. For nothing to be hidden, must each unique result be known in advance—that is, as soon as the methodic rule is applied to a specific circumstance? The answer must certainly distinguish between foreknowledge that there will be a unique result which consummates the method, and foreknowledge of the uniqueness in all of its qualitative particularity. Only the former can appropriately be implied by "nothing hidden."

Must the *genus* of all results be wholly known, where nothing is hidden? The weaver of tapestries, it may be supposed, knows what a tapestry is, even if he does not know what each unique instance of a tapestry will be; and the arithmetician knows what an arithmetical problem is, even if he does not know what specific arithmetical problems will turn up, or what each solution will turn out to be. But on this criterion, there is no discipline without comparable antecedent knowledge. A graver consideration is whether it actually can be said that the weaver and the arithmetician know indisputably what may or may not fall within the limits of their methodic practice. Is it impossible for them ever to encounter doubtful, borderline, or obscure instances of a "tapestry" or an "arithmetical" problem? In order that such uncertainties should be eliminated, the rules underlying a discipline would have to be (*a*) wholly explicit, and (*b*) wholly clear, in their meaning. If (*a*) and (*b*) obtain, then perhaps it can be concluded that "nothing remains hidden." But as for (*a*), what assurance can there be that a method is in fact determined only by the rules officially recognized? How can it be guaranteed that no implicit rule is operative? Even if an additional rule were added deliberately to define the conditions of conformity between the relevant mode of methodic conduct and the rules previously established, it could not certify its own perfect explicitness, that is, its own independence of any other covert prescription.

As for (*b*), there can be no assurance that any rule is free from equivocality and vagueness. The scope or application of a rule is always to some extent indeterminate. The fact that rules of method may stem entirely from resolution and legislation rather than from generalized practice or tradition does not eliminate the possible pitfalls. For a man who devises his own prescriptions and who relies on his own intentions is yet not complete master of their content. Whether in fact anyone can be wholly the author of a resolution; whether, in other words, it is possible to produce resolutions absolutely *de novo* is questionable; for the framer of rules must at least perpetuate in his usage some of the signs that preserve intelligibility, or continuity with precedent meaning. But aside from this, we are not entirely in control of what emanates from us, any more than of what belongs to us—a heart, a stomach, an arm, or leg. Our intentions carry us beyond our immediate vision. We can embrace a number of practices to which an intention is pertinent, but not all the possible ramifications of this intention. We do not fully know what we mean because we cannot exhaust all the properties, nor even the full general character, of any perspective within which our judgments are made. Nor can we ever fully anticipate every embodiment of the conditions under which our rule will apply. These are the difficulties that inhere in the enactment of statutes and rules by parliamentary bodies. We are inclined to scoff at the looseness of rules which are socially devised, and to contrast them with individually devised regulations, mindless of the fact that initial decisions of procedure can be kept in force only through subsequent decisions, decisions which even at best cannot be entirely formulated in advance. Descartes's own rules for heuristic procedure are so loaded with vague notions, so indefinite in their purview, so resistant to expeditious practice, that sometimes they read like a mockery of method. They speak uncritically and complacently of "sure and indubitable knowledge," of reducing "involved and obscure propositions step by step to those that are simpler," of "separating out what is quite simple from what is complex" until the "absolutely simple" emerges as proper starting-point, of freeing a question from "every conception superfluous to its meaning." The ideas on which Descartes relies as the keys to rules for solving problems are the ideas which cry out most loudly for clarification.

Descartes's view of intuition has been plagued by longstanding difficulties, and these need not be recounted here. What it means for intuition to be a "way," superior to other ways, is puzzling enough, and more relevant. Intuition is described as "the undoubting conception of an unclouded and attentive mind"; it "springs from the light of reason alone." An intuitive conception (apprehension) as thus described is also an action or operation. Is it an action consisting of one step or of several steps? It cannot consist of several steps, because if the steps are related deductively, this violates the basic Cartesian principle that deduction depends upon intuition and not vice versa. Nor can the steps be related in any other manner without making intuition depend upon mental operations which for Descartes are less reliable than deduction. Intuition is therefore a way consisting of a single step. This conclusion Descartes himself innocently confirms, under Rule XI, by the statement that what is intuited must be "apprehended all at once, and not successively." Accurately speaking, not only does the way consist of a single step, but of a single indivisible step.

A greater if not queerer difficulty lies in the question how intuition is related to the "certain and easy" rules of which a method consists. Every method not only consists of rules; it requires the capacity of intuitive apprehension, without which it cannot function securely. The "certainty" of the rules would seem to imply their certification by intuition. But on the other hand, intui-

tion, as one way of knowing, would seem to require
rules of its own that distinguish it from other purposive
ways. A way without directions—rules of direction and
identification—would lead nowhere and be no way at
all. Now a rule or body of rules can hardly be contained
"within" the single step of intuiting. Are they somehow
anterior to it? But dependency upon (and hence conformity to) rule robs intuition of its immediacy and
its self-sufficiency. Does an intuition reflect or illustrate a rule, without direct dependency upon it? The
rule would perhaps prescribe a certain course of conduct for inquirers—that they pursue "undoubting conceptions." But a rule of this kind could have no effect
upon the actual content of such conceptions: it would
be a rule that extolled the virtue of a practice it could
not guide. Should we say that the intuition as such is a
kind of rule? To the extent that a rule prescribes, this
is strained: there is little sense to saying, in the Cartesian scheme, that an intuition prescribes. To the extent that a rule limits or directs, an intuition might well
be called a rule, since its effect is to limit and direct
the subsequent course of thought and practice. And
yet an intuition can direct only implicitly, whereas it
would seem essential to the Cartesian position that a
rule be explicit, rendered in discourse. Even if we take,
as rule, not each particular intuition, but the universally
repeatable act of intuiting, the difficulty persists. The
act as act, not being a specimen of discourse, cannot be
explicit in the sense required. Thus the internal structure of the Cartesian position makes it impossible for
intuition to be a way, which *as* way presupposes rules.
But the last straw is that, even if some sense could be

found in which it became possible, the consequence would be equally bad. For when we raise the question how the rules of a method are to be justified, under Cartesian standards, we are compelled to say that they rest upon intuition. Then to make each intuitive way of certifying rest upon rules which rest upon further intuitions which rest upon further rules is to force an uncompletable regress, totally incompatible with the Cartesian theory.

A "method of rightly conducting the reason" (to take the phrase of the *Discourse*), like any other method, consists of rules. The rules of rightly conducting reason would themselves have to be determined by reason. In the form of intuition, reason lays bare its own path. History and "experience," perhaps, provide the temporal occasion of rational insight. Intuition "springs from the light of reason alone"—so that ultimately reason guides itself with certainty by its own light. There is no actual contradiction here. The problem is merely that the whole idea of method as something relating to human activity has all but disappeared. If there is a method of rightly conducting the reason, it would seem that there can also be methods of wrongly conducting the reason. Yet if the latter methods are methods in the Cartesian sense, they cannot lead us astray ("By a method I *mean* certain and simple rules, such that, if a man observe them accurately, he will never assume what is false as true" [italics added]). There cannot, then, be a method of wrongly conducting reason. Reason and method are synonymous. No method, if faithfully pursued, can be unsatisfactory; for ultimately there is only one way. What is insufferable in all of this is not the contradictoriness but the consistency of the position.

The consequences inherent in a position like that of Descartes make it understandable why Dewey should say that "another name for method" is "intelligence in operation." [5] The Cartesian stress on perfection through rule is replaced by the appeal to resourcefulness as the ultimate preserver of method. Regularization and rule can result in servility, which is as inimical to method as is randomness. The Cartesian conception of method is aimed against the incompetency, the inanity, the sterile, opinionated inertia of men. The Deweyan conception is aimed against the inelastic pride of the methodic engine, the gulf between methodic success and fresh insight, the excessive dependency of the individual on permanent criteria. Dewey sees methods themselves evolving as circumstances of application multiply. Rules exist to be "followed," but rules in turn follow the requirements of contingent events and changing human needs. "Intelligence" arbitrates between the old and the new, resisting frivolous innovation but remaining alert to the possible decadence or bondage of prevailing "ways." Hence rules become policies, and no method can completely illuminate all that lies ahead. But the Cartesian ideal is by no means wholly antithetical to that of Dewey. Dewey at times speaks as if method were something to be acquired, in the way one acquires a craft, something by which one is enabled to disentangle and uncover secrets. It is almost as if he feared excessive individuality in the practice of intelligence, or as if intelligence might prove too free to leave room for discipline. In possible concern for the transpersonal integrity of method, he describes it as "the thing most worth winning" in the quest for knowledge. And in marriage of these two emphases—on method as acquired and method as wrought—he says, "The value of any cognitive conclusion depends upon the *method* by which it is reached, so that the perfecting of method, the perfecting of intelligence, is the thing of supreme value."

Long before Dewey, and in similar vein, Bacon brilliantly raised the issue of whether it was possible for rules to function as initial guarantors of heuristic success. "The better sort of rules have been not unfitly compared to glasses of steel unpolished, where you may see the images of things, but first they must be filed: so the rules will help, if they be laboured and polished by practice. But how crystalline they may be made at the first, and how far forth they may be polished aforehand, is the question." [6]

If the novelist and the poet may use methods that do not rest on rule in the Cartesian sense, do they enjoy the same exemption from "policy"? Despite its suggestion of elasticity, "policy" no less than "rule" implies a universal that is present in an indefinite number of particulars. The same is true of such ideas as "style" and "character." Yet, the universals that all of these ideas imply, do not necessarily need explicit formulation, as does "rule" in the Cartesian sense. What a policy in each case embodies may be articulated subsequently by the critic, the historian, or the psychologist. Policy, like style and character, and unlike rule, need not be present at the outset of methodic practice, in the role of a device requiring conformity. The poet and the novelist, and everyone methodic, exhibits a policy in the course of his activity, whether or not he "has" a policy or "has adopted" one. To say that a method exhibits or even reflects a policy when practiced, is much less misleading than to say that it "rests" on a policy. A method rests on a purpose, which relates to consummation. A policy is an inclination toward activity of a specific kind; it gains its identity primarily by recurrence in methodic instances. That policies are likely to be vaguer than rules there is no need to doubt. What is of greater importance (we shall argue it again in a later context) is the fact that a vague policy, a vague methodic "direction" (in the sense both of an inclination and an aimed movement) can often be more desirably productive than a precise one.

For Coleridge, we saw, method and groping are opposites. This is equally true for Descartes. In the one view, an inspired impetus toward growth moves irresistibly to fruition; in the other, a luminous rationality predisposes the course of methodic events. What Bentham calls "chance" he considers to have no place in method but only in invention. All three of these conceptions exclude the position just suggested, that a vague direction may not only be methodic but of greater methodic value than a precise one. Now a vague policy or direction entails groping; but it is necessary to locate this idea in relation to randomness and to chance.

Randomness in human activity may prevail on different levels and is subject to degree. When it obliterates purposiveness, it is the prime enemy of method. In this respect it is dereliction, signifying blindness to goals, or at least apathy toward the possibilities of the future. It is tacit acceptance of non-control and sloth. On a particular level, however, randomness may itself be a technique or stratagem of method. When, for instance, we pursue random sampling, the general framework of purposiveness has dictated a specific form of non-control in the interests of discovery. Perhaps the general spirit underlying any such strategy of non-control is what the author of *Moby Dick* has in mind when he says, in Chapter 82, "There are some enterprises in which a careful disorderliness is the true method." Thus the mason who accepts the striations of stone and the dark burns of brick in the context of his products, and the woodworker who tolerates knots in his wood, carefully provide latitude for aberrations in the medium.

Randomness (except as a particular stratagem) represents the indifference of man to the transformability of natural complexes. Chance represents the indifference of nature to the methodic aspirations of man. Since human indifference is a species of natural indifference, randomness is a species of chance. Indifference, to be sure, is not necessarily hostility, and so chance can work for gain as well as loss. A "solution," says Descartes under Rule X, "can often be found without method." But relying on happy accidents, though strictly speaking a contradictory outlook, may be akin to a policy, and quasi-methodic. Descartes observes that faith in luck "is likely to enfeeble the faculties and to make people accustomed to the trifling and the childish." Chance has no unique relation to method, since it can be present anywhere in human existence.

Methodic groping is a kind of comradeship with chance—a conditional alliance. The fact that this comradeship is asymmetrical and humanly instituted in no way impairs its reality. For the favors that chance bestows are bestowed freely, and the gains by man are as great as any other of his gains. To maintain the alliance, the methodic agent requires only alertness and strength of perception. In a sense, the profoundest of methods, those of the sciences, the arts, and philosophy, depend upon the alliance most heavily. Their practitioners in fact, if not in principle, acknowledge perpetually that these methods can be extended or perfected. Each instance of practice contains an element of contingency and obscurity which only a desire for new insight can surmount. This element of contingency is a trait of the method, and not merely of the method's particular conditions.

No inventive process can be said to obviate groping on the part of those who engage in it. For every direction is vague in some degree when it starts with the prospect of uniqueness and unknown value in the product. Method that promises invention is query—the human effort to make the interrogative temper bear fruit. A good method for query does not mechanize effort; it only permits imaginative power to take form. Nor does it necessarily minimize effort; it only makes more likely greater substance in the reward. Method by itself cannot abolish the recalcitrancies of existence. Descartes's faith notwithstanding, no method opens a door through which one need only enter. Method does not provide a way already made but part of the equipment to devise a way. The best methods attempt to fight vagueness of direction, but not to simplify query. Were there nothing hidden in query, the interrogative temper would be a jest, and each method would be a surd or miracle. Groping, therefore, far from being, as some philosophers believe, the sign of weakness in a man or a method, is the price that the finite creature is naturally obliged to pay in the process of search.

The Cartesian point of view, influential in so many ways, prompts consideration of a formula in Kant. The penultimate paragraph of the *Critique of Pure Reason* contains a statement which is brief, stark, and vigorous. The similarity that it bears to the approach of Descartes lies in an emphasis upon method as carrying out a mandate, or as conforming to an intellectual requirement. As the keynote in Descartes is rule, so in Kant it is "principle." "If anything," says Kant, "is to receive the title of method, it must be a procedure in accordance with principles *(nach Grundsätzen)*." Now if "principle" were indeed meant to refer to any fundamental beginning or point of departure, if it were intended as the initial context within which a method becomes applicable, and if it were further intended as the complex of traits whereby each instance of methodic activity becomes recognizable, there would be little to quarrel with. A method, like every other manifestation of being, has its characteristic conditions. But a principle to Kant (omitting consideration of its precise epistemic function) is at least a proposition—a proposition of a foundational kind. And this makes the requirement "in accordance with principles" puzzling.

Does it mean that a method must explicitly follow a direction described or summarized by a universal statement? Such a requirement is not only arbitrarily limiting and "intellectualistic"; it also tends to confuse possible self-scrutiny on the part of a method with the purposiveness of the method. A method must have a typical aim. But it need not either articulate itself beyond the barest minimum or conform to a prior determination of its course. Explicit adherence to a charted path implies a self-conscious formulation that is altogether gratuitous so far as a practitioner is concerned. Formulations of this kind are much more relevant to the philosophic analysis of methods as practiced than to methodic practice as such. It is fairly common to speak of philosophically (or "methodologically") defining the "principles" of a method.

Analogous to the foregoing version of Kant's requirement, but far more defensible, would be the view that every method is antecedently "epitomized" by its practitioner in some form or other, not necessarily propositional. Thus each dramatist, industrialist, or physicist envisions some outstanding trait in his activity whenever he is about to pursue it. This conspicuous representative trait binds the repeated instances of method together. It is a symbol of their kinship, and of their common purpose. But a symbol of this kind epitomizes informally and practically, and should be distinguished from a summary or formulation of essentials.

Does the Kantian requirement mean that a method must embody an implicit principle which is eventually formulated, though not necessarily in advance? Nothing prevents anyone from enunciating in propositional form what he deems to be taking place typically in a methodic process. But in this way of understanding the matter it might be more accurate to say that principles are in accordance with a method than that a method is in accordance with principles. The latter seems to imply constancy in the principles; the former, to imply variability of the principles in proportion to the actual modifications of the method.

Does the requirement mean that every method depends upon "assumptions"—in the sense that it takes a number of truths for granted in order to proceed as it does? The subject of such truths would not be the method itself but, instead, facts or patterns of fact which the practice of the method presupposes. To note this, however, is not to make a requirement at all; it is to note what is quite unexceptionable, namely, that all activity—non-methodic as well as methodic—takes certain things for granted in its world or relevant perspective. It would make better sense and be more exciting for the requirement to be that methodic activity, as distinguished from any other form, serves to render explicit the things it takes for granted. The only trouble with such an exciting thesis is that it is false: it renders non-methodic a vast number of purposive and generic activities, including highly organized types of propositional query.

VII

Man's being realizes itself in two exhaustive dimensions. In one it assimilates, receiving the impact of all that is related to it. In the other it manipulates, making impact on all that is available to it. The most rudimentary manifestations of method reflect the manipulative aspect of life. Not that human activity, even as activity, is any less assimilative than manipulative, or that the two dimensions are separable. The primordial acceptance of natural complexes in varying clusters characterizes each moment and state of the individual. Assimilation goes on everywhere in the realm of method, as it goes on everywhere else. There are complexes in the methodic situation which are not produced and which perforce are accepted to begin with. The tendency of methodic man, intoxicated by the results of his own efforts, is to forget that he has modified his materials and not created them. But it is primarily by reference to the world as influenced, rather than to the world as endured, that method may best be explained. Method arises when man comes to recognize himself as manipulative. He thereby discerns his elemental powers, the simplest and in a sense the most fundamental of which is the power to repeat, to repeat anything at all. He may require more of the world than is presently available to him. He also may require less: when beset by heterogeneous possibilities, he may seek fewer options, as one who is constantly in motion seeks rest and a single place.

The methodic impulse springs as much from zest, and even prodigality, as from need. Men not only need but want. Whitehead errs when he says that in its origin every method is "a dodge facilitating the accomplishment of some nascent urge of life," or "the discovery of a dodge to live." [7] Not all methods begin in so frantic or so utilitarian a climate. Many arise for the purpose of exploiting some complex of existence and not for the purpose of salving some condition of distress. Many are gratuitous by previous standards. If they arise from any need at all, it is the need to play. When method is associated with the demands of pressing circumstances, whether these take the form of urgencies or of simple urges, it tends to be regarded as invariably remedial— as designed to fill a void, correct a deficiency, or resolve a doubt. But not all methods are remedial. Some augment what there is no reason to be discontent with; some economize, some reorganize, some transform. It might, of course, be argued that every method is ultimately remedial because it is always possible for men to improve their present state; there is always something that men need, whether or not they are aware of this. Methods, however, are dictated not by possible needs but by actual aims. If a method does effect an improvement in a given respect, this may well be accidental, leaving more basic directions of improvement uncharted. It is possible to think of each method as seeking a greater degree of perfection. But the specific perfections of methodic activity are not to be confused with humane perfection. The perfection of robots, of lethal weapons, of nationalist solidarities fulfill the actual aims of men but not the superior hopes of man.

Man is the animal that tries deliberately to limit his world in some respects and to make it more abundant in others. Methods emerge from these experiential strategies of increase and decrease, accentuation and suppression, as well as from the simplest persistent attempts at qualitative change. Strategy and persistence do imply what they seem to imply, a type of universality or repeatable pattern that is produced intentionally. But far beneath this calculative level there is in each human organism an underlying, though not unmodifiable, strategy of existence, resting on the relation of its powers to the state of its world. Every individual tolerates in certain ways and maneuvers in certain ways, and the order immanent in all of these ways is the widest possible sphere of existence for him. The Ideal Biographer of any human individual would discriminate various natural complexes relevant to the account of his life as an individual. He would separate (not without difficulty, if he were as scrupulous as his ideal status requires him to be) such complexes from others which are not relevant to the account; and among all the relevant complexes, he would distinguish (again, not without difficulty) those which he could ascribe to the individual as agent from those in which the individual was merely involved. Of those which he ascribed to the individual—the individual's products—he would wish to determine the larger significance (for being an Ideal

Biographer, he would not be afraid of colleagues who insist that he limit himself to the "facts"). Leaving it to the Ideal Psychoanalyst to trace each product backward for its revelatory significance, its motive conditions, he would trace each forward to discover its substantive nature as an utterance. He would try to determine its role as signifying a partial version of the self's world. He would see each product—each blink, sigh, movement, feeling, statement, joining, sundering—as at least an incipient position or standpoint taken by the individual well below the level of awareness or intention. Some of these positions or standpoints would be miniature, random, or relatively isolated; others would be unmistakable ingredients of a position of greater magnitude, or themselves dominant centers of interpretation. Each product would be found to have both a manipulative and an assimilative aspect, but its meaning to the Biographer might necessitate stress on one or the other.

Now men who wish to render themselves more determinate in a particular respect are on the verge of method: they wish to extend or intensify some phase of their being as productive creatures. Having been implicitly defined by a motley of standpoints—that is, having inevitably, unavoidably, judged the world in discrete instances, each by itself barely visible and perhaps of small consequence—they look for a greater degree of pointedness and connectedness than they perceive. All men crave to gain, though not only to gain. They aim at the preservation or furtherance or completion of something, not necessarily at gain for its own sake and in disregard of its ultimate form. They want to gain strength, knowledge, priority over others, skill, humility, admiration by others, authority, money, salvation, satisfaction, faith. Thus aiming at gainful judgment, the methodic man rejects the scattered multiplicities of judgment. He subjects himself to curbs and restraints, whether in the form of rules or restricted spheres of interest. He learns to compromise and to hope, long before he is able to see or to prevail. By cumulative renunciation he sharpens himself in some direction. It is in this direction that he refines the power to gain; in other words, to produce consistently as he wishes to produce; or in still other words, to appraise and pronounce securely.

Men judge the world through their exercise of certain far-reaching functions. Each of these forms of manipulative life is part of a larger natural relation, though the larger relation may become intelligible by the discovery of the manipulative form within it. Method reflects man's response to an overabundant yield from his own functions, which intertwine and resist theoretic separation, but which are none the less distinguishable.

1. Men cannot help recording and anticipating the complexes of nature. They do this most obviously by naming, describing, and inferring. The essential function thus constituted is that of assertion ("saying"). It is ordinarily interpreted by the type of persuasion that it seeks to introduce. Method, when it supervenes in this sphere, links persuasion to corroboration. It aims, moreover, to turn corroboration into an impersonal verdict imposed by the very complexes which are manipulated.

2. Of equal significance is that human function which consists in the contrivance of qualitative complexes. Nature is here manipulated by a process of shaping ("making"). The shaping is consummated simply as the shaped: the contrived complex is valued for its sheer existence. It need only show its traits. On the pre-methodic level, it is interpreted by affective satisfaction in its being, or by hunger for its presence. Methodically, contrivance not only exhibits without ulterior commitment, but probes the depths of natural complexes with prepared devices, and perpetuates products through ever novel forms and occasions of assimilation.

3. Men contribute to patterns that are measured by their effect on the conduct and destiny of other men. (This is "acting" or "doing.") The kind of manipulation which thus results in the alteration of feelings and interests is commonly interpreted by degrees of social and individual approbation, including self-approbation. When it occurs on the methodic level, action becomes privately and publicly more legislative, as well as more relevant to both the beginning and ending of conflict. Approbation, becoming increasingly differentiated, becomes increasingly codified.

Each of these three essential functions of man—statement, contrivance, and action—yields a genus of products. The multifarious products that are necessarily the instances of one or more of these genera comprise the extent of human utterance. A comprehensive theory of the human process must provide a satisfactory threefold formulation, and must use it to represent the modes of utterance. The notions of assertive, active, and exhibitive utterance, which we have framed and developed elsewhere, help to discern the principal attributes of man as a productive being. With the fundamentals of the general theory we are not concerned here. It is pertinent only to observe that method is the constellation of factors within utterance which permits utterance to detect its own possibilities. The products of man are deployed by the methods of man in structures that tend to remove them more and more from the conditions of their origin and to confer upon them self-sufficiency. Method commingles products with other complexes toward the consummation of additional products.

A method is not something literally present to hand, or something possessed and used as a chattel. Bentham calls a method a "fictitious entity," as indeed he calls whatever is not spatio-temporally describable, and as anyone would call it whose sole approach to all natural complexes was in terms of "entities." Actually no complex, however particular and however easily identifiable, is ever totally possessed in the sense that it is wholly present for manipulation. There is nothing which we can totally create, predestine, or dispose. The minimal determinateness of a complex, the trait-cluster which we initially accept, is the very condition of manipulation. Unlike a rule or law, a method is not always most intelligible in terms of direct, definite formulation. But like a law, a method consists of more than any particular number of instances. From the fact that a man has devised a method private to himself, it does not follow that he commands the range of all its possibilities. To say that a man "has" a method, a method of making this or discovering that, means that he is able to prac-

tice it, and perhaps also that no one else has ever practiced it. In terms of comparative possibilities, he may
be its poorest practitioner. The "chattel" conception
thus rests on mistaken assumptions. And it is as misleading as any conception favored by familiar locution
can be.

To pursue a method is to submit to an order of utterance. (The "submit" is important; for all utterance,
methodic or non-methodic, occurs in an order, in the
type of order that may be called a perspective.) Moreover—and this is a quite additional consideration, not
at all implied in the notion of an order—the order must
continue to be available. The repeatable opportunity,
the renewable provision for practice, is what permits
that measure of control without which the idea of
method would be nonsense. The kind of control in
which utterance is made purposive and is steered, the
ability to utilize a "way," underlies control of natural
complexes at large. Control of utterance is thus what
is implied by the phrase that we used earlier, "tactical
control."

Let us approach the conception of the renewable order of utterance from another angle. Some methods
appear to be so limited and special, or so inconsequen-
tial by themselves, that they are called "techniques,"
the term "method" being reserved for what is considered to have a certain type of breadth. Other methods, on the contrary, are so great in scope that they
encompass not only techniques or subaltern methods
but methods of considerable independent significance.
The scientific method is an example. Including in its
scope the special methods of the various sciences, and

within these, techniques which themselves may be extremely intricate, it thereby includes both general and restricted methods of formulation, inference, definition, verification, and measurement. Each science is an order of utterance or judgment. The scientific method is the potential reproduction of an order whose processes of judgment are shared though differently exemplified by each science. The scientist, like every other human, but in his own manner, judges in so far as he embodies through products the processes of estimating and pronouncing—processes which are ultimately indissociable from each other. He is continually engaged in the determination of complexes as more or less, this way or that, of one kind or another. He appraises certain types of relations as being natural complexes which remain invariant, and appraises the conditions of these relations. The guiding principles of his activities as scientist are actually guideposts: they bound his communal perspective or order of utterance. Collectively they reflect a bundle of aims. So forceful has been the influence of these aims in particular, especially on Western society, that they are often equated with the aims of method as such. But they determine one perspective and not every possible perspective. The ideals of explanation and prediction, of rigorous observation augmented by progressively refined instruments, of factual evidence and mathematical formulation, are simply irrelevant in some phases of human life. Whenever these guideposts are adopted as the boundaries of activity, the scientific order is reproduced. The method is "usable" because they are adoptable.

Now a method may be bounded but not completely

bounded. It may have guideposts, but not everywhere. It may evolve and need re-bounding. It may be distinguishable from all known methods, and yet not fully known itself. How can it be ascertained where a given method begins and ends? What are its essential and its accidental factors? Except for the most highly regularized processes, the techniques of which have been molded with machinelike exactitude, these questions are difficult to answer. A method as comprehensive as the scientific method may never get to be articulated as fully as we might wish. It is unlikely that even a single instance of this method in practice can be safely demarcated either with respect to its precise beginning in reflection and action or with respect to its logical and moral implications. So far as the arts are concerned, the problem of distinguishing between what relates and what does not relate to the practice of a method can be settled only by an abstract and highly conventionalized approach. The testimony of artists themselves in this kind of problem is ordinarily too anecdotal. So far as philosophic method is concerned, the problem of its limits and essential traits has become a vexing, disproportionate one in the twentieth century. The unqualified phrase "philosophic method" is intended to represent a core of procedure running through various schools, traditions, and individuals. There is no reason why such a core cannot be defined and periodically redefined, even in the face of great historical diversity. At the same time, nothing is more precarious than the attempt to isolate something known as pure philosophic discourse from the anthropological, poetic, programmatic, or biographical elements that are likely to be present in the same context; or the attempt to decide when such elements are separable from the philosophic process.

Can a method be independent of all other methods in the sense that its conduct is uninfluenced by the character and conduct of any other? Sometimes it is said that the method of science depends on no other; that this method above all is self-sufficient. It would seem desirable to say instead that the scientific method does not depend on any other method of truth-seeking or assertion or predictive knowing—or whatever qualification best names the province within which independence is possible. For in the first place, it is by no means insignificant to note that the scientific method depends on constituent methods, of defining and experimenting, for example, though the dependence is reciprocal. In the second place, there is an indefinite group of methodic conditions in the life of the human organism which are necessary for the existence and pursuit of scientific method, despite the fact that these too are never free of reciprocal influence. They are, for example, the methods of combining and separating sign-complexes, of distinguishing greater from lesser generality, of making and applying valuative comparisons. Methods of this kind, flourishing humanly outside the domains of formalized disciplines, are not ordinarily designated by labels. But they are genuinely methods—powers of purposive manipulation—regardless of the miscellaneous auspices under which they are employed. To contend that they are themselves phases of scientific investigation is untenable. Plainly, they underlie other methods than the scientific; they are necessary conditions even of methods which are antithetical to it in spirit. To make them tacitly scientific is to lapse into the view that there is only one method, of which all other alleged methods are forms, distortions, or aspects.

What is the status of a method when it is not actually practiced? It may "exist" in the form of written rules, physical instruments, models, memory images, or traditional records of conduct. Or it may exist in no concrete form whatever, as is likely to be the case with the methods of philosophers and literary artists. But at both extremes a method has the reality of a power. A power may be described as a possibility that has been actualized in some degree and can be recognized as generic in the next instance of actualization. A method cannot be reduced to a prior body of rules or instruments. These do not motivate and do not direct themselves. They possess an inert universality that has value once conditions and intentions bring them into a situation. Nor can a method be reduced to a prior body of ideas and sentiments. These are materials of method, sometimes the sole stimuli, but ubiquitous. They are wayward as well as purposive. The power in which a method consists may be found in a single man only, or in thirty men, or in all men. But it also may not happen to reside in any particular man or in any particular community of men. A method of altering international relations, or the scientific method of acquiring knowledge, or a method of educating the young, are each, as powers, indefinitely distributed and shared. The emphasis that is sometimes placed on the might of a method as compared with the limitations of its practitioners makes perfectly good sense. Power resides not in agents purely as such, but in a natural complex that embraces agents and other component complexes. ("I confess," says Locke, "power includes in it some kind of relation.") [8] When we speak of "man" we necessarily assume typical conditions that are indispensable to his being, a set of particularities that are congenial to it, and a range of contingencies that will promote or retard it. The fact, therefore, that methods are human powers does not imply that they can be exhausted by men, or that any one of them will be adequately fulfilled. There is no way of knowing whether any power, even a method of smallest scope, is exemplified as perfectly as it might be; for although a man may develop the powers that he has, and they may be rightly called his, it may remain uncertain whether in fact he activates them completely.

A method is not any kind of human power but a power to manipulate complexes characteristically within a perspectival order. The common expression "the power *of* a method" refers to the methodic process as an influence. It is the further power that belongs to man once his manipulative possibilities are realized in a specific form of (methodic) activity. We should distinguish, then, between the power to accomplish something deliberately ("a method") and the power of an actually practiced method to engender subsequent effects, effects of moment in other perspectives. Ordinarily, when one man says that he does not like another's method, or when different men agree that some methods are better than others, it is not of powers that they are directly thinking but of activities. Nevertheless, a reference to powers is correlated and unavoidable. The activity that is the subject of appraisal is tacitly seen as the effect of a power; for disapprobation of a method is more than disapprobation of specific instances of activity, and it continues in the absence of instances. A bad method is a power that is ineffectual or misdirected or used undesirably. When criticism concerns itself with methods and not solely with products, it either commends or reproves a pattern, and hence the power accountable for the reproduction of the pattern. Criticism that assumes a hortatory function, and prescribes socially, espouses the cultivation of powers that augur invention.

The notion of power is disguised in other forms. For example, when we speak of "discovering a method," we think we want to "find a way" to accomplish what we want. A specific destination is assumed, and the challenge is to reach it. But "to find a way to . . ." is clearly "to develop a power to . . ." In seeking method we wish, not simply to complete this operation or that, but to be able to accomplish a completion repeatedly.

To call a method a "way" or a "means" is usually an inaccurate or, at best, an elliptical version of the truth that a method entails the presence of ways and means, and the power of choosing and utilizing them. It no less entails the presence of ends, and the power of approximating them. There are non-methodic as well as methodic ways and means. When one is said to "find a way out" of a situation, the "finding" may be casual, or accidental, or frenzied, or anything else than methodic. Nor is the "following" or "pursuing" of a way enough to imply the presence of method. Men may follow or pursue blindly, madly, uncontrollably. A mere way or means may be something resorted to uniquely. It may be this particular way instead of that one. It may be not only unprecedented but useless from that time on—a mere happening. It would thus be extrinsic to the (methodic) requirement of renewal. To discover a method, then, is always to find a way, but the reverse is not true.

Sometimes methods are described not just as means (as being instrumental) but, more specifically, as instruments. If this is unsatisfactory, it is not because instruments have to be directly designatable articles like chisels, microscopes, or brushes. Theories, foreign trade pacts, and political parties have also been regarded as instruments, though for better and worse reasons. It is rather because the description turns a universal property into an instance of itself. Methodic activity is what permits products to be instruments. It is a necessary condition of all instruments, whether of making, saying, or doing. A method is no more comparable to theories than to chisels, being instead dimensionally related to each in so far as each functions purposively and recurrently. There is a difference between an instrument and that which functions instrumentally (or simply and circumstantially as a means). We may regard anything humanly manipulatable as functioning instrumentally whenever it happens to take on the property of mediating between one natural complex and another. The stricter cultural designation "instrument" is applied and limited to what is deemed a human product, and to what is not only *intended* as instrumental, but intended as *primarily* instrumental. Rivers and bees are frequently instrumental, but are not instruments in either of these two respects. River dams and bee houses are instruments in both respects; they represent a methodic use of rivers and bees.

A method, then, necessarily entails the use of means (it entails instrumental activity); the converse is not true. The use of means which are also instruments necessarily entails the presence of a method; the converse is not true. Since a method or power can be thought of as itself a product (see pages 31–32 above and pages 139–40 below), there is nothing really contradictory in anyone's looking upon such a method or power as ultimately an instrument in human affairs. It only amounts to saying that a power of manipulation is regularly manipulated. And this awkward idea is quite possible, except that it is a little like calling the family, or language, an instrument ("an instrument of community," "an instrument of communication"). The subject wears the breeches, but is too large for them. The usage encourages distortion and oversimplification of the nature of method, as the analogous usages do, of the nature of the family and language.

When method is thought of, not in terms of its own necessary characteristics, but in terms of the contingent role that it plays in a man's life, it may easily be a means and not much else. For example, it may be an object of study, considered only because it is required by another object of study. Likewise, it may acquire the status of an end in itself. And it may acquire this status either by being a primary object of study or by being cultivated as a principal value. Thus, to the philosopher of scientific method, the process is of greater interest than any of its products. To the financial adventurer, the process of making profits is of greater personal value than the profits themselves. In each case the methodic process (as studied or utilized) may be self-justifying. In another and altogether familiar sense, the scientist (not the philosopher of science) who is concerned with specific problems (rather than with his own method) as the direct object of inquiry may nevertheless regard the method as an end in itself, to the extent that pursuit of it, over and above each instance of its productive success, commands his primary allegiance. In none of these cases, of course, is the method literally separated from its results. Every method entails a characteristic result, that is, a type of result. Power, activity, and result are all factors (among other factors) included in the conception of method. On the other hand, inquiry and preference may be primarily directed to the parts or to the whole—to this or that phase of a method, or to a method in its essential form.

Where interest in a method ceases to be merely primary and becomes militantly exclusive, where regard for a method begins to be related inversely to regard for its results, a peculiar type of problem arises, belonging to the sociology and ethics of query. For this kind of inverse relation has as eventual consequence an erasure of the sense of connection between activity and its aims. The uses and fruits of method become objects of disdain. Methodolatry enters the scene, and methodic activity becomes transformed into a continuing proliferation of conventions. Methodolatry is more of a cultural than an individual problem. That certain individuals should focus short-sightedly is sometimes necessary, and contributory to invention. But that masses of individuals should do so implies social attrition of the alternative course. Men afflicted with methodolatry become self-righteous, and in their euphoria fancy themselves to have acquired unsuspected health. Methodic activity is identified with cultist works. Virtuosity is mistaken for originality. The epidemic colony turns into a reformist party which sees itself as correcting the extravagance of the old loose ways. In time, the aridity of correctness becomes evident, even to the faithful. The methodic imagination craves to be utilized and fulfilled. Procedural tricks prove meager fare, and the epidemic is broken, at least until new and more provincial methodolaters threaten to seize the day.

VIII

How specific must be the goal which is pursued methodically? In actual practice, almost any degree either of specificity or of indefiniteness may be found. A painter may direct his method to the attainment of an end so much subject to the demands of envisagement, and consequently so definite, that almost any of his products must fall short of the mark. Another painter may regard his method as efficacious even if it yields a large number of unanticipated results. A boxer who aspires to win regularly does not regard himself as lacking in method simply because he cannot always anticipate the way in which he will win—by an early or a late knockout, by a predominance of caution or of daring. On the contrary, his breadth of purpose may imply more intricate methodic control than if he aimed to win always in one way. Every method necessarily makes allowance for differences in the result to the extent that it recognizes natural resistance in the circumstances. Undesirable results, however, are attributable either to a failure of the method or to unsuitable conditions in its use. Which of these interpretations is the more valid in any particular case is among the perennial issues that confront purposive activity; and the factors leading to the adoption of one or the other interpretation are psychologically and socially complicated.

A purpose is not less of a purpose when it is vague, or more of a purpose when it is precise and its outcome is vividly anticipated. The man whose purpose is simply to build a house, though how and of what type he is unclear, is not aiming in the same way as the man whose purpose is to build a specifically planned house in a specifically planned way. But both factors of the former's purpose, his intention and his object or end, may be stronger: his end more firm, his intention more compelling. Likewise, a method with an indefinite purpose is not less of a method than one with a precise purpose. An arbitrator appointed to settle a dispute between two parties may employ a detailed, well-established method, though this may leave him quite uncertain of how the settlement will come about or what form it will take. Yet it is entirely possible that this type of methodic situation should develop more satisfactorily than one in which the various factors are more determinately present. The contingencies in the situation, the openness of the outcome, may challenge inventiveness; though it is scarcely to be concluded that they must do so or always have.

Many methods come into being in order to facilitate or simplify the attainment of an end. But to facilitate is not an essential trait of method. Altogether apart from methodic practices, there is no evidence that men always or even predominantly want to make things easier for themselves. Risk and speculation are not ways of minimizing effort; and yet risk, speculation, dissent, and deviation are frequent in methodic purpose. Technological methods are widely associated with the idea of making life easier. But the competitive, histrionic, mobile creature of these methods seeks anything but a simpler life with paler alternatives. Facilitating the attainment of an end may jeopardize the value of the end. In methods of manufacturing, of instruction, of psychological and medical therapy, a distinction is always apposite, between assuring attainment and expediting it. The easier way may affect the stability or durability of the result. The role destined for the result may make the harder way more appropriate.

A sharp distinction must be drawn between the two possible methodic motives of facilitating and economizing. The less economical method may be by far the simpler and easier to practice. Thus the loose colloquial formulation of a truth may be more easily utilizable than the economically formulated abstraction. A rambling, indirect, digressive way of narrating an event may facilitate practical communication, while an economically narrated account may strain response and impose arduous discipline. A method which employs redundancies and irrelevancies in the attainment of its objective may surely justify itself by the success of its function. Who is to legislate the possible values of method? The association of method with the idea of economy is widespread, both in popular belief and among practitioners. Hobbes at one point identifies method as "the shortest way." [9] Economy is important for mathematics, natural science, and philosophy, though in descending degree, respectively. For the methods employed in such areas as journalism and teaching, it is on occasion imperative and on occasion disastrous. In the arts it plays no necessary role, and often is meaningless as a consideration. Nor does it play any more fundamental a role in the literary arts than elsewhere. It can be made intelligible as a factor in the method underlying *Madame Bovary,* but not in the method underlying *Gargantua* and *Pantagruel.*

The consciously manipulative man develops aims commensurate with his powers. He develops methods also for the appeasement of pre-existent aims. These methods preserve the aims which provoked them. They encourage the survival of expectation. New aims breed new methods, but the methods bred render the aims more definite and less novel. By and large, the older an aim, the greater the number of methods it is likely to breed, or at least to seek, assuming, of course, that its importance is in more or less direct ratio to its age. Additional methods may fire and intensify old aspirations. Methods, then, are modes of being which preserve and universalize the needs, wants, hopes, whims, and ideals of man.

It seems worthwhile to distinguish between the aims which a method as such embodies and subserves, and the aims which reflect the values of its practitioner. The methods of a store clerk embody the aims of making as many sales and winning as many purchasers as possible. But these aims inherent in a limited (methodic) perspective may be repugnant to him within the broader perspectives of his life. The schoolboy who despises his lessons may accept the aims imposed upon him and employ the methods necessary to attain them. For method employed under duress (not simply out of need) is as common, and quite as methodic, as method "freely" devised. The cripple, the prisoner, the taxpayer methodically aim to alleviate their lot. The process that each utilizes is as purposive as any other methodic process. Regardless of the compulsive conditions of the choice, it is one among a number of possible choices, and it is an alternative to confused or semiconscious or submissive existence. There is evidence enough that of the countless methods used by men an impressive number entail intra-methodic aims that are not representative of ideal aims. So methodic activity minimally requires little devotion and no love. One tends to assume that the major methods of man, those which have awakened superior men and had the greatest historical effect, could not have flourished on this minimum. But it is hard to know, considering the subtle historical interplay of social and psychological forces. Whatever the powers of individual men may continue to be when their own primal impulses have dwindled, cultural trends can curb invention of their own accord. And just as the major methods of man can be culturally and institutionally attenuated, the more limited, average methods can be invested with new life, pursued with robust assent and the full preference of the individual —the methods of growing orchids, brewing beer, cheating on examinations, betting on horses, preaching sermons, keeping files, subjugating minorities, flying kites.

Every method reflects a certain measure of audacity. It reflects a sense of renascent opportunity and a rudimentary feeling of potency. Considered purely in its beginning, in relation either to an innovator or an adopter, and in abstraction from aims or consequences, method is strikingly human, signifying rejection of the mere particular occasion. Audacity or daring at first seems to be far removed from this spirit of reproduction; it brings to mind unique action, deviation from regularity. But these latter traits are not only consistent with method; they are best realized by it. For the most effective deviation from regularity is the establishment of another form of regularity, and the most important kind of unique action is the kind that becomes stabilized and reproductive of its instances rather than the kind which, though spontaneous, is evanescent. The methodic man preempts something of the future. He is able to build without having to build once and for all. He is willing to be tried repeatedly by circumstances. When his method succeeds, he acquires mastery of a sort. This immanent human impudence is not to be confused with the excrescent boldness of bomb-makers, charismatic personalities, or fervent optimists. Such as these are likely to be obsessed by the idea of "dominion" over "nature," which has somehow always clung to the idea of method. The idea of dominion is a good vague one to play with, say on a cloudy afternoon when men are incarcerated by a few inches of snow. Out of the domestic daring of the humbler methods, and the humbler masteries that stem from their practice, eventually come the labors of inventive judgment and the masteries that dignify mankind.

Thus the advent of method, in social history or in an individual life, always reveals a spark of reckless spontaneity, whether for good or ill. But the subsequent cycle of methodic activity can occur within a wide range, varying from the extreme of habit to the extreme of pure query. These extremes are not of equal significance. Coleridge tells us that methodizing may become habitual, that there should be habits of method. What he is thinking of, however, is a "habit" of living, one which, by its own activity, does not usurp methodic activity proper but continually re-introduces such activity. Even so, "habit" in this context actually means inherent moral policy or human inclination, part of the experiential framework within which method functions. The habit of adopting methods is thus quite distinct from the evolution of a method into a habit. Within the pursuit of an end, pure habit is ultimately the death of method: it strangles discretion first, and then obliterates the memory of purpose. When the gradual transformation of method into habit assumes social form, it can become a trend with crucial effects. For example, the historical growth of industry brought with it the elimination of discretion from the methodic contribution of the worker. Here the social career of one methodic complex varied inversely with that of another. The metamorphosis of the worker from a craftsman into a factory operative, which meant the substitution of training for regularized feeling, went hand in hand with the opposite movement of industry into new directions of methodic resourcefulness. The processes of the factory worker could remain methodic, even as those of the medieval commentator upon compilations of dogma could; for manual routine, like intellectual routine, did not yet have to be sunk wholly into habit. The relative degree of ingenuity possible for the operative of orthodoxy was incomparably greater. And his methodic direction was not, in general, inverse to the methodic direction of religious history. But his predestined role represents an equally marked instance of the progressive habituation of method, the grooving of the path.

Method becomes inventive when it takes on the property of query. Query is that form of human experience which originates partly in a compound of imagination and wonder. It is exemplified by philosophy, by the inquiry of pure science, by art, by what remains of religion liberated from the proprietary conception of belief, and by any number of informal but not undisciplined human processes which express themselves in some purposive pattern of utterance. Although query occurs only in a methodic framework, its traits are not reducible solely to methodic traits. The fact that a process is methodic expresses the purposive functioning of human power in an order of judgment. But the fact that it is a process of query expresses more than the (methodic) ramification of the judgments involved; it expresses their indefinitely continuing ramification. Query is more prodigal than method as such. For although it necessarily represents utterance moving toward some end, it luxuriates and complicates. The primary effort of method is repeatedly to complete its instances; of query, to deepen each instance. Method without query can destroy mankind and its own laborious progeny. Method informed by query is the essential expression of reason. Reason is query aiming to grow and flourish forever.

Query, however, does not refrain from seeking consummation. On the contrary, it can hardly exist on vanity and is incongruous with pride. The interrogative spirit requires products, steps to further heights. But method reminds men of the terrain and the law, seeking recurrent relatedness between a means and an end, leaving it to query to innovate, and tempering query by providing universality. Method may produce apathy. Query may mourn, but it cannot live with apathy. Method can be indifferent, and can serve any cause. Query implies a type of moral direction.

IX

What is the relation between method and knowledge? There are methods of acquiring knowledge, methods of suppressing knowledge, methods which yield knowledge though knowledge is not their primary aim, and methods to which the idea of knowledge is irrelevant. Looking the other way, knowledge may be acquired methodically or non-methodically. And non-methodic knowledge may be acquired either purposively or accidentally. Consider a man whose purpose is to know why he is feeling uncomfortable. He finds that all the windows in his house are closed. He opens a window and answers his question. He has made assumptions, and he has observed and inferred, but more as a matter of isolated occasion than of method. A man who stumbles happens to discover that he has injured his ankle. He has increased his knowledge without even having sought to know. Others, as the saying goes, come to know without even knowing that they know. Whatever is attempted, whatever occurs, may have cognitive effect. But some attempts yield knowledge of a fertile, distinctive kind. Distinctive and pursuable kinds of knowledge may be yielded by methods of making and doing as well as by methods of saying, though the latter profess to yield it more frequently than do the former. Method in any mode of utterance may succeed or fail in a specific cognitive aim which it may happen to have.

But if not all processes of method necessarily aim at knowledge, and if the acquisition of knowledge is not necessarily methodic, must it be said at least that each and every power of acting methodically presupposes a kind of knowledge appropriate to itself? No, not each and every. Some methods presuppose knowledge only in the sense that merely being alive does. Their practitioners must know something about the conditions environing a plan. A methodic power also depends on other powers, and on constitutional endowments. Above all, a methodic order always presupposes a more comprehensive order within which the aims that govern method arise. A method may be a method primarily of doing or of asserting or of making. But the more comprehensive or generative order, the next up, so to speak, in the concentric succession of experiential orders, is likely to be a tangled cluster of doings, makings, and assertings. The cluster as a whole has a cognitive value for the individual or group embarking upon methodic operations, and it will have an effect willy-nilly. But depending upon the nature of these operations, the cluster may be diffused in its effect or specially accentuated. The historian may draw upon it as a cognitive fund directly for a cognitive end; the dramatist may draw upon it as a cognitive fund but not directly for a cognitive end; the engineer may distrust its heterogeneity and try to ignore it; the pole-vaulter, the bank robber, the deer hunter, the boilermaker may simply absorb it.

What is the relation between method and system, understanding "system," of course, as of human origin and not as an existential order or merely natural structure ("solar system," "circulatory system")? It is said of certain inventive persons that they are unsystematic; but it cannot thereby be meant that they are unmethodic. Socrates was methodic but not systematic. We can ordinarily say in what respect an artist is methodic, but it is difficult even to say what it means for an artist as artist to be systematic. The terms "system" and "systematic," then, are not interchangeable with "method" and "methodic" but name specific traits that may be found within the general span of the methodic process. These traits are of three kinds, depending on whether the primary subject of consideration is (a) the typical operations that lead to (or that actually constitute) a product, (b) the way in which a certain type of product is made to disclose itself, or (c) the way in which different products are made to relate to one another.

To be systematic in the first respect (a) is to go about one's purpose by a number of steps each of which can be justified in both its function and its serial location. Steps which are systematic need not be final but only plausible and conditionally justified. A theorist or an artisan is not felt to be unsystematic merely because he reverses his ground or revises the succession of steps he has taken. He need only aim at the most desirable succession that method allows in a particular situation. So far as (b) is concerned, system seems to imply an emphasis upon fluent sequentiality as well as a vague feeling of appropriateness. Thus the mathematician is felt to be systematic par excellence, each successive component of his reasoned product commanding approbation. A similar feeling obtains in the case of the natural scientist's authenticated result, and in the case of philosophies like those of Aquinas and Spinoza, where firm schematic devices sustain the flow of reflection. On the other hand, where methodic movement in the product appears to be obscured or wilfully interrupted (Plato) by myth, soliloquy, unreconciled directions of argument, and digressive analogy; or where it appears perplexingly fused (Kierkegaard, Nietzsche) with paradox, private life, and immoderate expression of emotion— the properties of system are considered absent.

In the foregoing respects, then, system is a quality (*a*) of style or manner in methodic activity, and (*b*) of internal sequence in certain methodic products. In the third respect, (*c*), system implies a concern with varied products or results of methodic activity—specifically, with the linkage of relatively self-contained results in a pattern designed for greater substantive fruition or deeper communication. But the pattern or scheme must be one that is both intended and accomplished, since any sum of results whatever will of itself necessarily fall into a pattern of some kind. Thus Socrates and Plato, at least ostensibly, are not concerned with a schematic interrelation of their results, and are not systematic. Leibniz and Peirce are much concerned with such an interrelation, though they fail to carry it out: they are systematic in intent. All theoretical scientists are systematic in intent and in effect: they seek to interrelate as many results as possible in an inferential scheme. Kierkegaard and Nietzsche are concerned with reiterating the results of their methods, but not with systematizing them in the present sense: there are any number of leading themes, but no schematic interconnection of these themes. Methodic results that are distinctively patterned may be patterned gradually; the linking may evolve. Thus what is called "the jury system" is the institutionalization of a method, a scheme binding the results of a ramified legal process. But in such a case, it is well-nigh impossible to isolate intent, and to say what individual or what collectivity of individuals is "systematic."

Those artists who frame an inclusive structure for their products might perhaps, without undue strain, be called systematic. Instances of such a structure could conceivably be the *Oresteia,* the *Human Comedy,* the vault of the Sistine Chapel. But the notion of system remains more uncertain in art than elsewhere. Leave aside for a moment the requirement that a systematic linkage be an intended one, and consider the question of what is in fact accomplished. Why, for example, should we not regard all the works of Mozart as parts of a grand musical system? Conceding that a total life output can hardly be designed to constitute a single structure, it is still worth asking what there is in the mutual affinity of Balzac's novels that makes it allegedly of a firmer or more cohesive kind than that of Mozart's compositions? Would the interrelation of the latter have become different if a collective name had been assigned? Is the continuity of persons and events in the *Oresteia* a more "systematic" linkage than the general cultural setting in Ibsen's social dramas, or than the framework of ethical experience in the whole of Greek drama? The systematic linkage of products is to be carefully distinguished from the realization of a broad purpose. The latter is the looser and more comprehensive notion, and if it alone were the criterion of system, Nietzsche would be as systematic as Aquinas. The most persuasive manifestations of "system" in art are those undertakings in which several types of schematic device reinforce each other. The linkage of Michelangelo's Sistine paintings is, as it were, tightened by biblical epic, by physical juxtaposition, and by decorative architectural function. And yet even in this case, it seems less useful and significant, less obligatory, to speak of Michelangelo's projects of painting as systematic than to speak this way of, say, Kant's three "Critiques."

The relation between method and system can be seen from another slant. What are known as deductive systems are methodic orders of inference ultimately characterized by a specified number of symbol components and a specified number of rules governing organization and practice. But different systems, for instance axiomatic geometry and the propositional calculus, may exemplify the use of one and the same method, such as the formalistic method. And on the other hand, one and the same system may serve as a means of analysis for different methods, such as the formalistic and intuitionistic methods. When we speak of a philosophic system we are not necessarily identifying any particular philosophic method. Two philosophers with different methods may both be systematic, and two philosophers with the same method may not both be systematic. Thus Spinoza and Kant, using different methods, are equally systematic, notwithstanding the more easily identifiable type of sequentiality in Spinoza's system. Heidegger and Kierkegaard are basically similar in their method, though the former can be said to be systematic in a way that the latter can not.

There are stubborn and persistent conceptions of the systematic which are not the less arbitrary for their long standing, and which have gone far toward making the term "systematic" generally precarious. One of these occurs in connection with philosophic thinking. A philosopher is often called "systematic," regardless of the kind of sequentiality within his work, and even regardless of his use of results, if he deals with a certain minimal number of traditional "problems" or areas of thought. To "cover" these problems, in whatever way (by whatever method), is to have a philosophic "system." At first blush the answer to the question who is and who is not thus systematic seems easy. But the identification of the "traditional problems" is not quite so easy as it is supposed to be. Plotinus and Descartes, for instance, would each be described as systematic in this sense. Yet it can be argued that the number of problems which they do not treat in common is far greater than the number which they do.

The particular issue of what constitutes a system in philosophy is formidable. Whether in philosophy or elsewhere, it seems clear at least that the character of the essential sequence and the linkage of results can not be established by nominal classificatory schemes. Nor is the systematic interrelation a terminal procedure, one that is separable from and subsequent to the unfolding texture of utterance. This consideration is of great importance. For with regard to philosophy it means that the linkage of results mirrors, or is at bottom, the conceptual linkage of diversities in the farthest reaches of human experience. The philosophic texture making for system needs both dominant and subordinate concepts. It needs a judicious number of generalizations of varying breadth. It needs strength alike to solve problems and to portray natural complexes, whether these be anciently or newly discriminated. One frequently stipulated condition is that the components of a philosophic system must be "organically" or "internally" related. But it is perhaps better to acknowledge the large number of forms that the interrelation may take, and to stipulate the coarser yet difficult condition that the components actually be components—that they ascertainably contribute to the attainment of a gross objective. The concepts and generalizations, the assertions and portrayals, must all be helpful to one another, and must all conspire to extract imaginative assent from the assimilator. For miscellaneous analyses and solutions placed in physical proximity do not make a systematic order even in so historically charitable a domain as philosophy. The components, when understood in their own limited terms, should make evident what the gross objective will be; and the objective, when independently formulated, should make the components convincing.

To link philosophic ideas by weaving a formal inferential apparatus around them, is not to be philosophically systematic. Selecting a word that has had something of a philosophic history—"value," for instance— then erecting a purely syntactic and deductive framework for it, accomplishes an exact elaboration of intended meanings; but it is not a philosophic "theory of value." It is a complex definition that may prove to be useful when certain categorical or ready-made formulations are sought. With or without a formal apparatus, every philosophic system is a broadly inferential structure: certain implications, after all, are present, others are not. Such a structure is implicitly required when it is specified that problems, concepts, and generalizations be of varying scope, and that they be given the status of components.

In certain fashions of philosophy the attention to system wanes almost in proportion as the attachment to a specific method waxes. From time to time, systematic thinking is abjured and condemned, with no concern for the question whether it is of a better or worse variety. Sometimes the condemnation is spiced by a gracious maxim that breadth is what is really needed in philosophy. But apparently breadth and system must never go together, since actual attempts at the achievement of breadth are inevitably labeled (to use a current idiom) "woolly" or "pompous." The solution of problems, we discover, reduces to the critique of all proposed solutions, or else to the separation of solutions from each other. There is pathos as well as irony in the fact that so many of the plaintalking-clearthinking-hardhitting-levelheaded celebrities of philosophy prove to be mere exponents of a new propriety, and loud in their detection of sin. There is greater pathos in the fact that at bottom they want more than anything else to be systematic, and to excel in the directions which they find themselves to be denigrating as archaic.

What is the relation between a method and a methodology? The latter term and its verbal relatives are far from constant in their meaning. It would seem natural to say that in the broadest sense "methodological" questions are those dealing with methods as their subject matter, questions pertaining to the origin, scope, nature, and relative value of methods. But this does not undo certain entanglements. The particular expression "a methodology" sometimes designates the "rationale" of a method, in the sense of a body of stated or tacitly understood policies developed by practitioners of that method. The policies may arise from the need to reflect and epitomize past methodic experience, or from the need to clarify difficult methodic instances. Whether, in this sense, a methodology merely reflects methodic practice or legislates to methodic practice is a thorny question that should be pursued in close connection with study of the history and development of particular disciplines. From one point of view, any group of accepted policies, however passively accumulated, exerts prescriptive force.

There is another sense in which the expression "a methodology" designates the rationale of a method. The rationale is assumed to be a kind of structure inherent in the method rather than a set of policies or strategies relating to its conduct. Hence it needs exposure. In this sense, a methodology is the "theory" or "philosophy" of a method, the attempt to chart it or interpret it not merely in terms of its putative goal or the interests of its practitioners, but in terms of its relation to other methods and to other human considerations. It is to philosophers, therefore, rather than to practitioners, that the exposure or formulation is assumed to belong. Philosophers of science sometimes are inclined to think of their province as "methodology" —not just as "a methodology" or "the methodology of science"—despite the fact that they are actually concerned with one method and its special forms, and despite the fact that they may not even be concerned with all of the fundamental aspects of that method but only with the "logic" of its operations.

The expressions "a methodology" and "a method" are often used interchangeably. Expositors make loose allusions, all intended as parallel, to historian A's "methodology," sociologist B's "method," anthropologist C's "methodology," economist D's "method." Perhaps the emphasis underlying the equation is upon method as conscious of itself, as formally aware of its operations. But methodic practice, though necessarily aware of itself as purposive, is not necessarily aware of itself dispassionately and critically, that is, of its own structure and comparative status. A method as such, we suggested earlier, need not articulate itself otherwise than through its cumulative career of situations. The problems that confront a method, methodic problems, are not necessarily methodological problems. The former are concerned with the actual, effective exercise of a power, with the attainment of results, either generally or in a particular instance. The latter are concerned with the detached, uncommitted understanding or analysis of what thus takes place. One methodological problem would be to articulate the nature of given methodic problems.

When disputants brand one another's methods as unsatisfactory, weak, poor, or dubious, they are taking a common end for granted (even if it be only the production of useful results), and are referring to what they regard as unpromising means to this end. Since the concern with means is of great importance, the criticism will ordinarily express itself in terms not just of what is "methodically" or "procedurally" or "technically" unsatisfactory, but of what is "methodologically" unsatisfactory. The latent intent is to stress the magnitude of the difficulty, as against a mere inadvertence in strategy. The still stronger expression "methodological error" is sometimes intended to lay emphasis upon the fact that the user of a method has misconstrued his own commitment. The charge in this case concerns not the choice of method but its practice: it is not the choice or selection that is "erroneous," but the use. The very same phrase "methodological error," however, is frequently intended to imply something else, namely, that universal laws of a discipline known as "methodology" have been contravened, with dire and general intellectual effects. Here the crime is more than mismanagement; it is presumably ignorance—though of what, one might well wonder.

It is interesting to reflect that the term "methodology," even when not actually used in connection with science, is most often used with the covert assumption of science as paradigm. When the term is associated with philosophy or theology, it carries the suggestion that these disciplines are sciences, if only in an extended or analogical sense. Sometimes one hears not just of the method, but also more questionably of the "methodology" of a craft, of business, of teaching, of administration. The phrase "the logic of method" applies to a realm of assertion, where principles, inferences, or predictions are paramount. Notions like "the logic of art" or "the logic of diplomacy" are based on a limited number of similarities to the scientific process, but in the last analysis bespeak the attempt to emulate an alien ideal. In these types of utterance—that is, in the realms of contrivance and action—when it becomes necessary to recognize the practitioner's discrimination of his methodic process and its aspects, it might be more appropriate to speak of a "methodography." The principal concern of the scientist in reflecting on his procedures is to guide further inquiry. By articulating rules and techniques he converts these into impersonal devices. The artist, however, prescribes only when he succumbs to weakness, or when he has nothing better to do. As distinguished from such dubious normative advice, his methodographic reflections are perfectly indigenous and have a threefold importance: they help him to detect the repeatable elements in his own practice; they are stimuli to the imagination of other artists; and they serve as data for the philosopher, who alone is in a position to venture on abstract comparative study. Adequate methodography is rare and difficult. The artist and the diplomat, to mention these only, are not at all confined to description in an anecdotal sense. They can observe what would otherwise be disguised and submerged traits of their practice, and they can do this without laying down universal rules. It is theoretically possible, if by no means usual, that they should be their own best critics, in the sense of articulating their own actual procedures. Moreover, each can discern similarities and differences between himself and others in the same discipline, and thereby contribute to a natural history of artistic or diplomatic activity.

Both a methodology and a methodography may be said to articulate methods. There are philosophers and practitioners who believe that this or that method is not subject to articulation, that it has the kind of uniqueness which renders it insusceptible to adequate formulation or description, or to illumination beyond its own actual practice. Omitting for the moment the question whether this type of belief misunderstands the nature of articulation, it reveals itself as a species of the belief that certain realities defy investigation—whether they be feelings or qualities or non-human occurrences or human occurrences or anything else that may have struck men as awesome and subtle. Now the claim that is contained in this kind of belief cannot itself be immune from investigation. It must at least articulate its own rationale. And among the accounts it must provide is one that explains the difference it has assumed between investigable and uninvestigable realities. But as soon as it ventures on such a comparison it contradicts itself. In the process of comparison it cannot avoid some determination of the existential status and peculiarity of that which supposedly yields no determination. Nor can it take the form of an a priori assumption that any determination yielded must prove unilluminating. For once yielded, a determination is (at least in principle) capable of increase. This turns the a priori assumption into a factual prediction, the baseless prediction that an indefinite number of possible attempts at illumination, all as yet untried and unknown, will fail. Moreover, any responsible prediction of failure would seem to require that the criteria of failure and of success be specified.

Somewhat different is the claim that the articulation of a method has no appreciable effect, or at least no salutary effect, on the practice of that method. The claim is not without merit when it is recognized as a limited generalization. The most common form it takes is the opinion that the philosophic study of methods does not influence the work of scientists and artists. There is reason to believe this. Yet, if the scope of the opinion is extended backward to a time when the distinction between scientist and philosopher was less sharp, when the arts were less isolated from other disciplines, and when professional specialization was less widespread, there is plenty of room for doubt. When contemporary scientists and artists undertake their own philosophic reflection, its effect on their methodic activies remains problematical. For there is always the notorious possible disparity between what the scientist or artist says and what he does, between his professed and his actual operations. On the other hand, useful as it is to note this possible disparity, and to warn against the facile identification of different functions and competences in one and the same methodic practitioner, each specific case probably deserves independent analysis. With respect to realms where methodic processes are more standardized, where the products of method are esteemed less for their uniqueness than for their abundance, efficiency, or social availability—agriculture, technology, political administration—the view that the articulation of methods has no effect on prac-

tice, is simply false. Historically significant changes of
method in these realms have resulted not from experiential trial alone, but from exposure and clarification
of the methodic processes as such.

Is it paradoxical that in realms like agriculture and
engineering, which are ordinarily less associated with
"articulateness" than is pure science, methodic practice
can actually be more responsive to articulation? Not at
all. And here it becomes important to understand the
general nature and purview of articulation. Once it is
perceived that articulation does not necessarily take
the form of discourse, that there are indirect as well as
direct forms of articulation, and that therefore articulation is not necessarily limited to methodologies and
methodographies, this problem and others appear less
stubborn.

The method of a poet, however difficult it may be
to formulate, is (partially) articulated whenever other
methods reveal its traits. It is articulated by its own
products, and by any other products that reflect its influence. The imitation of the method by disciples or
by parodists articulates it no less than direct verbal
criticism or direct "examination." Any form of articulation, far from being an all-or-none affair, may continue indefinitely, both in degree and in time. The
evolving attitudes of readers, auditors, or spectators
over a period of years, or the changing directions which
formal criticism may take, are articulative processes.
To claim, therefore, that a particular method is not
subject to articulation is virtually equivalent to claim-
ing that the method does not exist. The methods of pure
science can be articulated by methodological inquiry,

by ethical inquiry, or by non-discursive effects such as technological application. Profoundly different in spirit as pure and applied science may be, every application of a scientific principle contributes to the articulation of the scientific method. For it discloses one way in which the principle is exemplified, and in which the method of reaching the principle can yield consequences. The methodological observation "By their fruits ye shall know them" is designed to make both the good and the rotten fruit equally significant. Technology that is morally good and technology that is morally rotten alike articulate certain phases of the meaning of scientific operations. The traits that belong to the scientific method are to be sought not merely in this or that order but in every possible order which it affects. Every ramification in any way traceable to the method exposes one of these traits. Human uses which are to any extent dependent upon the functioning of the scientific method, to that extent articulate its nature. For although no use can be made of the method without some human decision, the decision by itself will not suffice for that use. The decision may require that method and no other.

In the attempt to understand the nature of a particular method, it is absurd to cite the good effects of the method and to ignore the evil ones. To regard the latter as accidental and the former as essential is a surprisingly widespread tendency. It sometimes takes the form of assuming that destructive applications of the method are actually "misapplications"—a term which obscures the fact that moral irresponsibility may be wholly compatible with methodic fidelity, and the fact that certain types of moral irresponsibility would be wholly ineffectual without the power conferred by the method. In the attempt to regard a method as wholly good "in itself," the most desperate expedient is to contend that all of its practical applications, all of its technological translations, are wholly alien to its nature. But if they are really "applications," and are alien to its nature, from what other nature do they derive? And what other method makes them possible if not this one? Human decision is as much part of a methodic process as of its eventual translations. What is called the objectivity or dispassionateness of a method consists not in its exclusion of human choices, but in its patterning, regulation, or guidance of these choices, its introduction of a compulsive dimension that excludes arbitrariness. This patterning or determination sets limits and opportunities for all human decision, practical as well as theoretical, and defines the possibilities of technological no less than of intellectual choice.

The heinous applications possible for a method of knowing cannot abolish the glory of pursuing the method disinterestedly and acquiring the resultant knowledge as an end in itself. But neither can these applications be dismissed from the company of all other data that articulate. They help to expose the possibilities that reside in the method pursued and the knowledge acquired. Part of the vast meaning that a method may have, as technological articulation in particular has revealed, is to be able to destroy the conditions of its own continuance. It is always possible, of course, to resolve by fiat that nothing shall constitute an articulation of scientific method but the discursive reflections of those who study language systems. Historical changes and social complexities, not to mention greater philosophic awareness, eventually show how puerile such resolutions are. A method of agriculture might once have been understood and clarified solely by the memory which farmers had of ancestral practice; but verbal rules about what shall constitute clarification cannot curb the spread of the method's revealing effects. For it may conceivably be articulated not only by theories of chemistry, but by economic relations, by the values of a people, by military developments, or by folk music.

X

A method is a power of manipulating natural complexes, purposively and recognizably, within a reproducible order of utterance; and methodic activity is the translation of such a power into the pursuit of an end—an end implied by the reproduction. This consequence of the foregoing considerations has already been stated in substance, and so has its basic justification. Its meaning is not dissociable from that of other conclusions developed in the general context which precedes and in the three final sections which follow. We are now in a position to make further observations about some of its constituent ideas.

1. Although a power may exist prior to given instances of its exercise, the designation of a power as a "method" implies an envisagement of activity. A method is separable from its use, but not from an awareness of possible use. The idea of a method inherently unusable is self-contradictory. A methodic power also implies prior activity, within which it came into being: the prior activity warrants its discernment as a power, and distinguishes it from an abstract possibility.

2. It is not quite accurate to think of methodic activity as the realization or actualization of method. For the

power as such is real or actual—it is different, for example, from the supposition or notion of a power. The activity is the "translation" of the power in a quite literal sense: both in the sense of a transformation into something else, and in the sense of a furtherance or conveyance of human purpose toward completion. Bacon uses the term "delivery" to suggest the nature of method. Method, he believes, is the provision of rules for the delivery of knowledge (or "knowledges").[10] But whatever it may be that method delivers, it does deliver in the most important traditional senses of the term: it brings (or delivers) offspring (good or bad); and it liberates (or delivers) one complex from conditions that resist transition, or translation, to another (good or bad).

3. The term "power" here relates not just to the prospective manipulation but to the prospective manipulation-within-an-order. It would be just as right to say that a method is a power of reproducing an order of utterance in which natural complexes are to be manipulated, as to say that a method is a power of manipulating natural complexes within a reproducible order. However, the same type of caveat would be necessary, namely, that the power is not just the power of reproducing an order but of reproducing-an-order-for-purposive-manipulation.

4. When the scope of the power is understood, the qualification "purposively" becomes redundant; for, strictly speaking, the reproduction of an order of utterance implies an end to which the manipulation directs itself. The psychological or rhetorical justification of the redundancy lies in the fact that the mere power

of manipulation as such, and the mere presence of an order, are rudimentary to the human process of experiencing, and do not in themselves imply method. (It is to be noted that, even following the specifications "purposively" and "reproducible," the phrase "pursuit of an end" does not become redundant. The emphasis is on "pursuit." A method implies an end, while methodic activity implies an end actually pursued. But to add "actually" to the formal statement is unnecessary: the term "translation" is to be taken seriously.)

5. Looked at in the light of the preceding point, the qualification "recognizably" also becomes redundant. The reproduction of an order brings with it the essential characteristics that identify the manipulation. An order of utterance, after all, is no blank state; it is an interrelation of judgments and natural conditions. But the presence of "recognizably" in the statement is a reminder that the instances of any method are bound to each other by appreciable similarities.

6. In whatever mode of utterance or judgment manipulation occurs—assertive, exhibitive, or active—that which is manipulated is a natural complex. Signs no less than their designata, principles no less than sensory contacts, human individuals no less than individual "things," are complexes of nature. Accordingly, theoretical assertions are manipulative no less than physical contrivances or moral actions; theoretical contrivances, no less than physical contrivances; inferential actions, no less than moral actions.

7. By an "order of utterance" we intend a "perspective of utterance." There is a strange custom of usage which is willing to place the practitioner "within" an

order, but not willing to allow a "perspective" elsewhere than in the head, the mind, the eyes, or the feelings. A perspective within which utterance occurs is a
structure of conditions under which men produce. It
is necessarily part of a larger perspective within which
men "experience." We have already indicated, though
indirectly, that the term "perspective" is by far prefer-
able on theoretical grounds to the wider term "order."
Mere order does not imply human existence, whereas
perspectival order does. The term "order" has such
inhibiting popular associations (e.g. "orderliness"),
which to boot are so uncritically and automatically
identified with method, that its use is a risk. The use
of perspective, with its own limiting associations, is of
course also a risk. "Order" is chosen for the present purpose because it has the advantage of being less cumber-
some where compendious formulation is desired.

8. An "end implied" does not necessarily mean an
envisioned end or a specifically preconceived end. Nor
does the "pursuit of an end" imply perfect determinateness of the end being pursued. As Dewey might have
put it, the pursuing influences the character of the pursued (as well as the character of what is attained). There
is always a generically recognizable end that belongs
to a given method. But this does not exclude surprise
and novelty, and in general, great diversity in the results.

9. Why should the order of utterance be a "reproducible" order rather than a "recurrent" order? Might
it not be argued that in certain situations the order is
visited upon or imposed upon the practitioners of a
method and not deliberately reproduced by them? Thus

fire and flood, to which methods of checking fire and flood pertain, are not wholly unexpected; but neither are they intentionally provoked. The difficulty here lies in mistaking the circumstances of methodic activity for the order in which such activity occurs. The confusion is made more likely by the fact that there are typical circumstances, and by the fact that any circumstances in themselves constitute an existential order which may be antecedent to the methodic order. Now an order of utterance, being itself an order of existence, is not separable from other orders of existence. Methodic activity does not choose its complexes *ex nihilo*. At the same time, to the extent that it is methodic, it represents a power which is anticipatory. This anticipatory power is precisely the power of reproducing a structure and direction for utterance. Thus fire recurs, but the order in which we cope with it (active utterance) is reproduced by us. The fire is successively part of two orders, one pre-methodic and the other methodic. The second overlaps the first. The order reproduced presupposes not any power at all but a power relevant to a specific kind of complex that may be. A fire is a typical circumstance for which an order of human judgment has been designed. Methodic orders are themselves modifiable, on the basis of many possible considerations, though sometimes by the passage of time alone. But each, as modified, becomes pertinent to a more or less identifiable range of circumstances.

10. To describe a method as a power does not exclude the possibility of its also being, in other respects, a product. (*a*) A power may be original relative to a given undertaking, or it may be developed, whether

imperceptibly or deliberately. Like other kinds of traits, it may be attained and cultivated, extended and modified. (*b*) A power may be formulated or institutionalized, thereby acquiring a measure of independence from any particular practitioner. It may arise as the product of other powers. For instance, the power to make various medical diagnoses is ultimately the product of the power to solve biochemical problems. (*c*) Methodic activity is the translation of power, but it is none the less the product of men who utilize the powers that they have.

11. The ideas of manipulative power and reproducible order of utterance facilitate recognition of the discretionary element in methodic activity, and help to define its place. Discretion is the primary source of variation within the rhythm of methodic activity. It is decisional manipulation, serving to mediate between power and circumstance, and between the typical and unique phases of circumstance. It is the steering function of method, compromising methodic uniformity, but by the same token saving method from rigidity and failure. In the Cartesian theory it is at best a necessary evil, a prop, lurking outside the proper domain of method. At the other extreme, in the Deweyan theory, it is inflated into intelligence, as if there were no other methodic factors determining its function. The Cartesian "rule" emerges as an inadequate counterpart of reproducible perspective. The Deweyan "intelligence" emerges as discretion exiled from its natural correlatives, perspective and power.

Whitehead speaks of a "Way of Rhythm" in nature. Limiting the notion somewhat, it seems justifiable to interpret each human life span as a fantastic network of rhythms, in all varieties of relation to one another. Where any of these rhythms originates in voluntary utterance, it takes the shape of methodic activity. Purposive judgments that are not methodic are indeed necessarily located in an order of utterance, but not in a reproducible order, and are therefore not part of a rhythmic pattern, except as mere natural complexes. Method is the rhythm of human purpose. The non-purposive phases of human life supply background cadences—the beats of the physiological functions, the ritual regularities of communal behavior. Within the non-purposive realm there are also cadences that are less bland, such as the undulations of desire and impulse, or the alternations of wounding and healing. The multiplicity of human rhythms is anything but harmonious. In one and the same individual the methodic rhythms may contravene the physiological and social, and tax them to the point of reciprocal curtailment. Methodic rhythms vary greatly in their degree of subtlety, precisely as do methodic aims and products. The differences may go hand in hand with other differences that carry ethical significance, but pervasive rhythm as such is no more than an existential trait within the human process, and unlike reason or query it is neutral ethically, as method itself is.

It is possible for a method to be so diffused and scattered in its operations, so remote from formal procedure, that its practitioners may not ever adopt it independently but discover themselves to be following it. Into this type fall the methods, for example, of acquiring belief and of governing action, that are linked with social groups and defined by tradition. Sectarianism of any kind may be methodic. Sectarian devotees may not have devised their commitment individually, or selected it purposively from among alternatives, but they may purposively retain it, feel loyal to it, and bind themselves to its regularities. The manipulative power they exercise, they may wish to continue exercising. Social devices for rite and sanction ensure recurrent self-consciousness even after dominant original purposes recede into the background. In this sphere a method reaffirms itself constantly. It becomes the true and only "way." It realizes itself periodically through its own familiar products, which are interpreted as its exemplars: the good citizen, the beatific personality, the hero, the leader, the public servant. It reinforces itself by exposing its deviants, those who lapse into unchastity or beardlessness or larceny. Innumerable other methods intersect it and coexist with it. With some of these it blends; with others, it is in a state of preserved belligerency.

There is a philosophic danger that methods of this kind should be construed as query. An element of quest tends vaguely to attach itself to authoritative sponsorship of the right and the good. The processes that refine protocol and doctrine appropriate the idea of perfection. That they have no resemblance whatever to inquiry, or to any science in particular, and that instead they have supplied some of the most powerful obstacles to inquiry, is beyond argumentation. But it does not follow that they exemplify other forms of query than inquiry, namely those in the realms of contrivance and action. Protocol defends the good, caressing it into submissiveness. Query discovers the good, endlessly defining its conditions. The machinery of taboos can be a model of method; with the interrogative spirit it has no necessary relation. To say "no possible relation," however, would be to overstate the point. The interrogative spirit, though not nourished by sectarianism and tribalism, may yet find nourishment therein. Inventive contrivance, independent action, and even inquiry have at times taken their point of departure from a doctrine, a myth, a deeply anchored custom. The human complexes within sectarian life, the natural materials that are reflected by it, are subject to transmutation by query, as all other complexes are. The methodic practices peculiar to sectarianism are not duplicated along with the sharing of its materials. Query does not seem to require the repudiation of even the most provincial loyalties. It tolerates alien and outlandish company. Nevertheless, it owes intrinsic allegiance to the deeper sources of its own life. It too depends for its practical continuation upon tradition, the many-sided tradition of its institutional embodiments such as art and science, and upon the sporadic inclination of human beings toward invention. These traditions and possibilities of man are at once its tributaries and the objects of its loyalty.

There are levels of activity, methodic in nature, which cannot be called social or institutional in the usual sense. Freud speaks, for instance, of "methods by which men strive to win happiness and keep suffering at bay." [11] Although the activities thus identified have a social dimension of a kind other than the kind which Freud acknowledges, he is not wrong in regarding them as ways pursued by individuals. These ways are as diffuse and spread out temporally as institutional and sectarian ways. But as pursued by individuals they may range from non-methodic directions of impulse at one extreme to query at the other. The vague expression "way of life" does not imply method any more than does "way" by itself. Sometimes it is to be understood merely as descriptive of the direction in which men happen to be moving and the predominant practice in which they happen to be involved. But at other times it is indeed to be understood as naming a direction purposively adopted. When sponsored by social forces, such a direction is likely to constitute method without query. When determined by individual intent, however, it is likely to constitute query in its most intricate and precarious form. It must embrace, within its area of manipulation, the most bewildering situations of man. And within its order of utterance it is committed not merely to action but to contrivance and assertion of the most laborious kind. The chance that it can be enduringly, not to say coherently, pursued is small. But before it is denied the status of an inventive method, by the temper of rationalized fragmentariness in the present era, there is some value in remembering that various peoples at various times have thought it not implausible.

XI

No philosopher of this century has been more closely identified with attention to method than Dewey. So far as the fact of the matter is concerned, attention to "methods" would be more accurate. Method never received from Dewey the direct and generalized examination that he bestowed, for example, on categories like experience and thought. For him the subject was part of a broad theory of ways and means, which underlay investigation into complexes as varied (and yet as related) as the educational process, social revolution, aesthetic response, freedom, mind, and religious experience. It is entirely conceivable that leaving the nature of method to be interpreted on an implicit level resulted in a more fruitful philosophic achievement than deliberate categoreal analysis might have permitted. It is equally conceivable that such analysis might have reduced the number of difficulties within Dewey's philosophy. In any case, a number of issues in this area of Dewey's work need to be uncovered for the purpose of furthering our own investigation.

A previous glimpse has revealed the key notion of Dewey, that method is synonymous with "intelligence" or "intelligence in operation." [12] (In certain writings he speaks of "*the* method *of* intelligence," rather than of method *as* intelligence. But the latter conception is what we discover when we look for generalized discussion.) "Intelligence" is the name Dewey gives to what he calls "directed operations," collectively constituting "inquiry," which solves problems, or which, in other words, eventually transforms unsettled, doubtful situations into situations that are determinate. Intelligence is also described as "a quality of some acts, those which are directed." It is "part and parcel of nature's own continuing interactions. Interactions go on anyway and produce changes. Apart from intelligence, these changes are not directed. When an action intervenes which directs the course of change, the scene of natural interaction has a new quality and dimension. This added type of interaction *is* intelligence." Dewey thinks of intelligence as the source of what is good and as a good itself. He goes on to say, "The intelligent activity of man is not something brought to bear upon nature from without; it is nature realizing its own potentialities in behalf of a fuller and richer issue of events. Intelligence within nature means liberation and expansion."

Sometimes Dewey refers to a method simply as a "means." [13] It is possible to weave together the broad, noncommittal notion of means with the notion of intelligent action by regarding intelligence as the capacity to select means for the achievement of ends. This, however, is quite different from intelligence as the capacity to solve problems. The process of solving a problem does imply the choice of a means to an end. But as we shall show, the process of choosing a means to an end does not necessarily imply problem-solving activity. When Dewey speaks critically of certain methods, for instance of "a method based on predilection for ultimate and unattached simples," [14] or when he says of a method that it "was imperious and impatient, but it served a need," [15] or when, in general, he says that "some methods succeed and other methods fail," [16] he is thinking of these methods simply as "means." If these methods are all "method" in the sense that Dewey himself has defined—if they are instances of "intelligence" —they are instances of intelligence as the capacity to choose means, but they seem obviously not to be all instances of intelligence as the more specific capacity to solve problems. There is no evidence that these two strains in the conception of intelligence, and hence in the conception of method, are understood by Dewey himself to be different. On the contrary, he treats problem-solving as co-extensive with the attainment of "consequences" by "means deliberately employed."

In most of Dewey's formulations, the two strains are uncertainly fused. Thus in the context where he describes intelligence or method as natural interaction "in behalf of a fuller and richer issue of events," he describes a man as intelligent "in virtue of his capacity to estimate the possibilities of a situation and to act in accordance with his estimate." Now the methods of Hitler illustrate the requirements for methodic action implied in this latter formulation. To Hitler must be ascribed "intelligence" in so far as he could, perhaps peerlessly, "estimate the possibilities of a situation and . . . act in accordance with his estimate." He could ingeniously select means to ends. On the other hand, he typically solved no problems but only destroyed or repressed the conditions under which they called for solution. The actions that he planned with the utmost deliberateness exemplified natural interactions as well as any manifestations of action could, though they were scarcely "in behalf of a fuller and richer issue of events" or of "liberation and expansion."

From a purely formal point of view, Dewey's undeveloped idea of the nature of method can be made coherent in either of two ways, though in either way difficulties still remain. The first is to acknowledge the presence of the two strains in the conception of intelligence. The "means-end" conception would be applicable to any method indifferently, and Dewey's statements that there are bad methods as well as good would be made intelligible. The "problem-solving" conception would be reserved for the methods deemed superior by Dewey. The difficulty persisting, however, is that "intelligence" as such would cease to have any necessary connection with interaction "in behalf of a fuller and richer issue of events"; and the cost of the amended view would be a weakening of the symbolic association of the name "intelligence" with the process of perfecting human effort. Secondly, we can insist on the eulogistic sense of intelligence and method, and deny that the activities of such as Hitler are properly to be called "methods." The difficulty in doing this goes beyond the fact that too many processes called "methods" both by universal custom and Dewey's own predominant usage would have to be "reduced" to something else. It is that in the dubious activities under question, traits which are fundamental in Dewey's own

analysis of method and problem-solving are also present: thus in the actions of Hitler there is the estimate
of the total situation, the deliberate framing of alternatives and eventual elimination of the unfeasible ones,
the perception of certain things as signs of other things,
and the elimination of indeterminateness or doubt
from the situation. There may here be no solutions
of problems, whatever "resolutions" there may be. But
this is only an indication that the conditions specified
by Dewey for the attainment of solutions are far from
being complete or unambiguous.

Actually, the identification of method with problem-
solving is in itself unsatisfactory. For reasons previously
adumbrated and to be developed through the next
section, philosophic and artistic methods, to mention
no other, do not necessarily entail the attempt to solve
an overall problem. The inapplicability of Dewey's
conception to actual practice among inventive disciplines is unfortunate enough. Over and above this,
it is plain that the legislation of superior methods does
not erase the methodic actualities of the devils on earth,
or of the emperors without clothes, or even of the cheap
little monsters of salesmanship and politics who come
close to fooling all the people all the time.

Let us look more closely into the relation between
method and problem-solving activity. For Dewey a
problematic situation is an indeterminate or unsettled
situation that is recognized as such and therefore sub-
jected to inquiry. When do we settle an unsettled situation? But perhaps it is wise to ask first, what actually
constitutes such a situation? Dewey always insists that it
is not we alone who are unsettled, but the situation as

such. This point need not be argued here. What is germane to the issue is that in any case a situation must be composed of an individual (or individuals) who makes choices, other natural complexes, and a number of actual and potential relations between the individual and the other complexes. It is not composed of less than this. Now a situation is unsettled in some respect (as Dewey himself points out), and not in every possible respect. In a broad sense, any situation can be regarded as unsettled relative to some possible change that may take place in it, and as settled relative to some change that has already taken place in it. Specifically, a situation may be regarded as unsettled when any of the following types of conditions obtain—whatever other types there may be: (*a*) When an individual does not know of any means to attain a given end; (*b*) when an individual does not know which one of a number of means he *must* choose in order to attain a given end; (*c*) when an individual does not know which one of a number of means he *will* choose in order to attain a given end; (*d*) when an individual chooses one of a number of means to attain a given end, but has not yet attained it; (*e*) when an individual chooses one of a number of means to attain a generic end, but does not know what specific end he will attain; (*f*) when an individual chooses one of a number of means to attain a specific end, but does not know what generic end his procedure will subserve.

For illustration, take the following six methodic situations: (*a*) A physician confronted by an unprecedented condition in his patient knows only that he aims to aid the patient, but cannot think of any applicable principle of approach. (b) A police officer aiming to explain a crime has reduced the number of explanatory alternatives to three, and must choose one of them. (c) An actor who knows how he will play his part does not know which of three equally satisfactory costumes he will choose to wear. (d) A sculptor aiming to make a bust of an old man has chosen wire as his medium, but must yet produce the effect of his choice. (e) A painter who has chosen one of a number of radical color combinations in order to produce a configuration is content to follow his developing inclinations, whether he be led specifically to an iconic or a non-iconic result. (f) A philosopher who has chosen the word "fact" for the specific purpose of "analysis," is not sure whether his generic aim, over and above discovery, is to discover pervasive traits of existence or to discover idiosyncrasies of language.

In each of these unsettled methodic situations a completion of some kind is intended. In (a), (b), and (c), the means is uncertain, whereas in (d), (e), and (f) the means has been selected. However, in the last four cases, (c), (d), (e), and (f), there is not necessarily a problem at all, despite the fact that the individuals concerned are aware of the incompletion. For we can hardly speak of a problem if the completion of an undertaking, whether of means and end or end alone, waits upon the mere passage of time, or upon the occurrence of an inclination, or upon eventual growth in perception. A task to be accomplished is not the same as a problem to be solved. There may be a problem for someone else who wishes to explain the mechanics or the significance of particular choices, but not necessarily for the chooser.

Examples (*a*) and (*b*) represent problems, because the complexes indigenous to the situation have inhibited as well as halted the efforts of the choosers to attain the end sought. Although all manipulation, and hence all methodic activity in particular, implies resistance of some kind, the kind of resistance in the methodic situations (*c*), (*d*), (*e*), and (*f*) is no different from that in activity which is entirely unplanned and non-methodic. In order that a problem should be present, the individuals concerned in any situation must at some point in the situation be arrested or frustrated in the completion of their end by situational factors independent of them. (To be arrested by factors "within" them would not make the particular situation at hand problematical.) The mere fact that an end is not directly envisioned creates no problem. If a question takes a long time to answer, or an action takes a long time to complete, this in itself does not imply frustration. Nor does the fact that a question is left unanswered or an action left uncompleted imply that the unsettled state of the aftermath is of a problematical kind. The answer and the completion might well have been regularized or gratuitous rather than unavailable. Though the choice must be relevant to the situation as a whole, the determinants of the choice may emanate from the chooser. Thus the actor may methodically choose his garb by closing his eyes and reaching for the first of the three costumes that comes to hand. The philosopher may decide that conditions at his university counsel emphasis upon linguistic study as the framework of his analysis. Once again, there may be a problem for someone outside the given situation who tries to explain how an end is pursued, but not necessarily for the individual who pursues the end. All of the foregoing situations, then, are deliberate attempts to turn an unsettled state into a settled one. All relate means to ends. All are characteristic instances of methodic activity. But not all are attempts to solve a problem.

What Dewey basically seeks to articulate is a particular method that he feels to be of incalculable importance. His historical model is of course the method of natural science, and from the ideal of its practice he tries to generate another and more directly ethical ideal comprehensive enough to provide for the continuity of science with philosophy, art, and common conduct. (This is what underlies the expression "the method *of* intelligence.") His allusions to method (as distinct from this or that method) are in effect allusions to what might have been phrased as "method in its highest form." "Intelligence" should read "beneficial intelligence." And "the capacity to estimate the possibilities of a situation" should read "the capacity to estimate disinterestedly, with everything subordinated to the solution of a problem." For Dewey is talking about a certain type of moral commitment, and mere sagacity, craft, or prudence are not enough.

Even as an ideal, Dewey's conception of intelligence does not suffice for all types of methodic discipline. The scientist, the engineer, need to "estimate the possibilities of a situation"; and so does the philosopher in one phase of philosophic activity. But for the philosopher in other phases of philosophic activity, this is not a need and may be irrelevant; and for the artist it may be actually undesirable. The purpose of the artist, even when he is justifiably said to be involved in an "inde-terminate situation," may be to explore or aggrandize one trait in the situation. In consequence he may neg-lect or obscure other connected traits and other possible aspects of the situation. He may focus not on what there can possibly be but on what there is; and if he, in com-mon with other methodic individuals, makes conjec-tures, these are conjectures that he seeks to embody, not conjectures that he is or feels himself required to warrant. If we were to look beyond practice peculiar to the scientific model of intelligence, the notion of esti-mating the possibilities of a situation and acting in ac-cordance with them would reveal itself to be cloudy as well as inadequate. In any situation, an indefinite num-ber of possibilities can be conceived, and there can be as many estimates, according to as many themes of esti-mation, as there are men to estimate. Clearly it is not Dewey's intention to accredit any kind of estimate as intelligent, nor any action proceeding from any given estimate. A limited genre of estimates is favored and presupposed by him. Whether those who estimate non-problematically and act in non-resolutive ways are "in-telligent" or not is matter for debate. But they surely may be methodic creatures.

XII

There is a faint but deceptive analogy between Dewey's view of method as intelligence and Whitehead's view of method as a special manifestation of "reason." [17] Whitehead is impressed by the evolution and competition of methods. He sees methods as basic human attachments to ways of living. They come into being as imperative innovations. They claim allegiance, come to dominate, and hang on doggedly after their vitality and human value is ended. Their careers start with promise and conclude with the most tenacious orthodoxy. Temporally speaking, every method has a limited value. Human conditions, needs, and ideals inevitably change, and methods must give way along with everything else. There is a "natural human tendency to turn a successful methodology into a dogmatic creed." The scientific method, Whitehead believes, now represents an entrenched orthodoxy comparable to that of religion in an earlier epoch. Here, of course, he reaches the extreme of difference from Dewey, for whom science, as the historic embodiment of intelligence, represents precisely the ideal of perfect flexibility, being by definition no more capable of dogmatism than fluid intelligence itself. Whitehead lays much greater stress than

Dewey upon science as an institution, and upon scientists as unwitting instruments of epochal forces deadly in their cumulative influence. Whereas to Dewey the scientist is the dedicated servant of intelligence, to Whitehead intelligence can be the local and historical product of scientists, men commonly if not individually unaware of the philosophic presuppositions and the moral implications of their practice.

According to Whitehead, methods are engendered not by reason in an unqualified sense, but by the "practical reason." In its practical function reason discovers and clarifies "methodologies." When it thus "renders purpose effective," it "lulls itself with self-satisfaction." The "speculative reason," on the other hand, is not "concerned with keeping alive. It seeks with disinterested curiosity an understanding of the world. . . . It fulfills its function when understanding has been gained. Its sole satisfaction is that experience has been understood. It presupposes life, and seeks life rendered good with the goodness of understanding. . . . In this function Reason serves only itself." Speculative reason, seeking "the general reasons beyond limited reasons," is essentially "untrammeled by method." It seeks to "understand all methods . . . by transcending all method." This infinite and unattainable ideal is what makes men human. Practical reason has its basis in the animal needs of men. And yet speculative reason is not anarchic; it is "itself subject to orderly method," even though it is committed to no method in particular. We "now speak of the speculative Reason in the place of Inspiration." Actually there is an "interplay of the two functions," speculative reason providing the "theoretical understanding" (or "theoretical activity") necessary for the advance to new methodologies, practical reason providing the raw material for speculation. Science "has been developed under the impulse of the speculative Reason, the desire for explanatory knowledge." Basically, however, the difference is between rational operations "governed by the purpose of some external dominant interest" and rational operations "governed by the immediate satisfaction arising from themselves."

It seems that for Whitehead there are three stages in the career of any method, reflecting the general functions of reason to enable men "to live, to live well, to live better." Method first yields "a dodge to live." It "satisfies the immediate conditions of the good life," and then its middle period may be either a relatively long enrichment of life or a quick relapse into "mere life." A method which does not evolve "adventure" gradually declines into a monotonous stability. It ceases to reflect reason. "In the stabilized life there is no room for Reason. The methodology has sunk from a method of novelty into a method of repetition. Reason is the organ of emphasis upon novelty."

Whitehead speaks as if there were a few methods all in all—options for man. There is the "reigning method." There is something new which "the species seizes upon," something "beyond the scope of the old dominant way." The choice affects human evolution. Momentous consequences ensue. Reason is fulfilled or threatened. Civilization and barbarism confront each other. For Dewey the terms are different but no less oversimplified. Instead of acknowledging innumerable methods on innumerable levels, with varying degrees of relevancy to one another, devised by men with different kinds of intelligence aiming at both beneficial and destructive ends, and by as many men who must be counted enemies of reason as by its friends, he sees only a single scale ranging from intelligence or method at one end to helplessness, darkness, or vested interest at the other. Whitehead, thinking of all method as initially designed to satisfy the conditions of "the good life," loses sight of the fact that the beginning of a method's history may foment irrationality quite as much as its senile inertia may. If one wishes to think of reason as promoting the good life, one cannot think of reason as reflected in all methods.

"In the stabilized life there is no room for Reason." But are there not better and worse forms of stabilization? What if the basis on which the stabilization is achieved happens to be the practice of art and of inquiry? Or do art and inquiry necessarily require instability of life? Does stability entail complacency? Does reason not try to preserve and perpetuate the good as well as to find it? Is it not one of the functions of reason to separate the stable and recurrent from the incidental and contingent phases of whatever is found good? Does not adventure itself require stabilization if it is to be distinguished from mere transition? Must there not be a distinction between adventure as the novel impetus and understanding as the consummation? And does not understanding, therefore, even more than adventure, require stabilized knowledge and constancy within human experience?

"Reason is the organ of emphasis upon novelty."

Novelty of any kind? Novelty for its own sake? If reason emphasizes innovation, must there not also be recognition of the fact that many kinds of innovation either aim to undermine reason or in effect obscure its ideals? Is reason perhaps to be understood as that which keeps pace with a trend in the universe, a trend toward desirable change? Should we say that whatever newly becomes, subserves the purposes of reason? Should we not think of speculative reason as capable of detaching itself from change in order to appraise any instance of change?

It is not easy to understand what Whitehead means by "a method of novelty" and "a method of repetition." The gross import of the context seems clear enough. Methods can deteriorate from inventive processes into sterile rituals or habits. But an inventive method does not deserve so poor an appellation as "a method of novelty." Is such a method one that is somehow in behalf of novelty? Is it a method that is not necessarily in behalf of a novel end but novel only in its use of means? Is it a method that yields results each of which is novel or only the type of which is novel? And what is "a method of repetition"? All methods, inventive and routine, good or bad, are repeatable as methods. Does it make sense to say that some methods aim solely to accomplish repetition? But repetition must be either of some process or of some result. Are some processes repeated in total disregard of an end? If no end is sought, can we speak of a method at all? If a given end is sought repeatedly—if similarity of results is what motivates the method—then the value of the method is to be determined not by the mere occurrence of repetitions, but by the kind of repetitions that occur, and by the perspective in which they occur. Both repetition and novelty are compatible either with uninventive method or with method informed by query. Novelty by itself is not enough to introduce the interrogative temper. On the other hand, the utmost regularity in method may serve as a vehicle of query. Thus the most firmly established procedures in mathematics, the most highly traditional forms in poetry and music, the most deeply rooted of customs in moral action, may be instrumental to invention.

Can it be plausibly maintained that repetition is unimportant in the affairs of mankind? For Whitehead, repetition seems not even to express the practical function of reason. Innovation actually expresses both the practical and the speculative or higher function. The view is a strange one. For the factor of repetition is absolutely indispensable to both the practical and the speculative reason, as indeed it is to every aspect of human experience. The signs that men use, from the simplest index to the most intricate symbol, require repeatability as their primary condition of being. Without repetition, the continuity of meaning vanishes, as does any possibility of identifying and recognizing the most elementary complexes of existence. Out of the human need and desire for repetition there develop methods whose very justification lies in the exactitude or fidelity of the repetition and in the promise of its longevity. We want each copy of a printed book to be an exact repetition of the original, and we prize the method of printing that prevents any innovation. We want the drugs that are manufactured to be in each instance chemically faithful to the formula—to repeat the formula with no innovation whatever. Meaningless or irresponsible repetition can obviously have undesirable effects; but it is a fair question whether there is any difference in principle between repetition and innovation so far as the possibilities of evil effect are concerned.

Disparagement of method simply as method seems, on the surface, to mean defense of purposelessness, and of the eccentric position that floundering may be better than planning. Sometimes it is only a cloak for the repudiation of particular methodic forms. At other times it is based on a covert identification of all method with fastidiousness, or with economy. But the carefully qualified disparagement one finds in Whitehead derives from his conviction that method should be sought and pursued up to a certain point, beyond which something more fundamental, more fundamentally human, must be encouraged to thrive in complete freedom. A related type of qualified disparagement is to be found in Bacon, who similarly looks upon method as a potential threat to the expansion of thought. For Whitehead, however, the antidote to method lies in a higher function, speculative reason; whereas for Bacon it lies in the cultivation of "aphorisms" and "observations." Whitehead's speculative reason transcends method; Bacon's aphorisms precede it. Bacon feels that method is often in danger of being developed prematurely: "Knowledge, while it is in aphorisms and observations, it is in growth: but when once it is comprehended in exact methods, it may perchance be . . . accommodated for use and practice; but it increaseth no more in bulk and substance." [18] So for Bacon method suggests the ripe and the terminal; but for Whitehead, the green and the primitive. "Aphorisms, representing a knowledge broken, do invite men to inquire farther; whereas Methods, carrying the show of a total, do secure men, as if they were at farthest." [19] Very much like Whitehead, Bacon depicts complacency and stagnation as eager mates of ingenuity: method suffers too much from its virtue of stability, and it poses the greatest dangers when it reaches the peak of its worth.

Bacon must have meant his generalization to be a rough one. That men are frequently stimulated by "a knowledge broken" and rendered complacent by "the show of a total" is true enough. But men have also been stimulated and inspired by the example of the completed process and the effective method. Perhaps method weakens the weak and strengthens the strong. And the very same can be said of aphorisms: these too, and possibly more often, have been known to "secure men, as if they were at farthest"—as if each parcel of thought were ultimate and perfect. Bacon's contrast of methods and aphorisms reflects a confusion of method in general with system in particular. The more plausible contrast would have been between isolated insights (aphorisms) on the one hand and linked or concatenated results (system) on the other. Method may yield either type of products. The notion, however, that aphorisms or observations have independent meaning and independent validity prior to any systematic context is an error into which Bacon sometimes (definitely not always) falls. That aphorisms are not independent of method in general, and themselves reflect methodic activity of some kind, is suggested by Bacon's own

larger framework of inquiry, which approaches the subject of aphorisms in terms of "diversities of method."
But in Whitehead, the possibility of purposive discipline independent of method is categorically affirmed.

Whatever value there may be in Whitehead's version
of the distinction between speculative and practical reason, the distinction itself is of small help in understanding the nature of method. What is more, it contributes
to the survival of egregious errors. Whitehead is saying
that the practical or "methodic" function of human
reason is to organize living, to find ways, to anchor and
guard the essential underlying processes. The speculative function is to gain "theoretic understanding" and
"explanatory knowledge" for its own sake. Speculative
reason is the philosophic spirit. ("The whole conception of philosophy as concerned with the discipline of
the speculative Reason, to which nothing is alien, has
vanished.") In seeking "the general reasons beyond
limited reasons," it has provided and must continue to
provide progressive, flexible guidance for all other disciplines, including science. And since "we now speak
of the speculative Reason in the place of Inspiration,"
it seems fair to conclude that all inspiration is ultimately philosophic insight. This would have pleased
Coleridge—at least as much as Whitehead's tendency
to make inspiration supersede method would have dis-
pleased him.

What shall we say, on Whitehead's principles, of the
method of Shakespeare? Is it an expression of the practical reason? In the usual senses of "practical" the idea
is ludicrous; but in Whitehead's sense, especially ludicrous. For to him practical reason "works in the se-

cure daylight of traditional practical activity. It is the discipline of shrewdness." Is the method of Shakespeare, then, less truly a method than an effusion of speculative reason? In the sense of "inspiration," partly; but there is nothing speculative about it in the philosophic sense. It most certainly yields understanding, but it neither aims at nor produces "theoretic" understanding. It yields knowledge, but it is not employed to produce "explanatory" knowledge. It is a fertile stimulus to the philosophic imagination; but it reflects no insight into "categoreal notions" or into "abstract schemes of morphology," which to Whitehead are the essence and splendor of speculative innovation. The plain fact is that the functions assigned to reason by Whitehead, whether to practical or speculative reason, are virtually irrelevant to the inventive methods of the arts. To the non-linguistic arts this irrelevancy is especially striking. The general, and wholly unacceptable, consequence of the view is that art is no sphere for the operations of reason. There is thus no way of explaining the nature of method in art, or even of acknowledging its existence.

Serious as this consequence is, there is another that is equally serious for Whitehead's conception of philosophy. To the extent that there is no formal recognition of the methodic processes within art, the interpretation of philosophic method must be incomplete and partially distorted. Philosophy is kin with art as much as with science. Ironically, Whitehead, who thinks of science as having moved increasingly in a self-contained direction, as having repudiated what it needs most, namely philosophic speculation, interprets philosophy as concerned ultimately with "the content of belief" and the production of tenable propositions—in effect, as science fortified by comprehensive intuitions. That the categories and affirmations of philosophy do indeed require and deserve warrant, that they can maintain themselves as assertions in an involved but compelling rationale, is one of the many important emphases in Whitehead's work. It is an emphasis that resists the general degradation of the discipline, and the infectious sense of defeat in the face of experiential complexities.

But Whitehead's account is only half-satisfactory at best. For the categories and formulations of philosophy have another function. They shape an order which in itself serves to judge without contending or declaring. Each such order, through the unique interrelation of its conceptual components, uniquely identifies and selects natural complexes which would not otherwise become available. For any who become able to share and utilize the order, it is possible to grasp what would not otherwise be grasped. What is grasped may range from traits of great scope that seemingly suffuse everything, to traits that reside in small hard corners of existence. Aquinas, Hegel, G. E. Moore, each show as well as tell. In so far as they pursue their own variation of philosophic method, a specific direction of query, they cannot help showing uniquely, whether it be types of ontological interdependency, properties of thinking and believing, or a particular realm of discourse. What philosophers show will be different, even when what they say coincides. An exhibitive dimension, in and through the medium of general concepts, is implicitly expected in a philosophic structure; it may be neither expected nor prized in a scientific theory. The idiomatic and the unique, which are fundamental in exhibitive utterance, are basically irrelevant in a product of science. It is misleading to ask whether what is exhibited is a structure of "ideas" or a structure of "existence." All judgment, whether it take the form of action, contrivance, or assertion, manipulates by ordering natural complexes and endowing them with a recognizable identity. To presuppose the "in-the-mind" versus the "in-the-world" issue as inevitable is to misunderstand the nature of judgment and to confuse the kind of utterance inherent in making with the kind inherent in stating. The philosopher perforce exhibits a structure of concepts, as the artist exhibits an auditory, narrative, or visual product. He perforce manipulates one or another part of the world. He "changes the world" to the extent that he modifies its relation to himself. His perspective, the concepts that reside within it, and the meanings generated from his contrivance, constitute a natural complex intimately related to non-human complexes.

The exhibitive function in judgment is to be distinguished from the iconic function of a "sign." An iconic sign designates something through likeness. Maps, photographs, and, in general, all diagrammatic or mimetic devices designate by reproducing the structure or the particular qualities of their objects. (In exhibitive utterance, designation plays no necessary role. Whatever the medium of exhibitive utterance, linguistic or otherwise, the judgment consists in the product. The product may happen to be interpreted as designating, either iconically or through symbolic association; but it may not.) A philosophic theory that "shows" certain characteristics of existence need not, as a body of signs, reproduce or resemble these characteristics. To show is not necessarily to duplicate. One man can show another what he means by pointing to something rather than by reproducing it. But he can also show by providing the means for another to look and find. Philosophic concepts and conceptual structures are exhibitive mainly in this last sense. They fortify the resources of the conscious assimilator. We spoke earlier of a philosophic structure as portraying natural complexes. The present elaboration should make it clear that the species of portrayal implied is somewhat analogous to that given by the narrator of events or the analyst of a political situation, and very remotely analogous to that given by the photographer or the mime.

It is the exhibitive function that is alluded to when it is said, with respect to an established language, that certain properties are lost in the process of verbal "translation." What the language "states" is statable in another language with suitable elements. But what the language "shows" cannot strictly be repeated from another vantage point. (This is not to be confused with the question whether it can be articulated from another vantage point: it can be progressively articulated from many vantage points, and in any of the modes of utterance.) In a philosophic as in a cultural language, the vantage point is unique. The power of the language to show is shared best when the language is adopted, rather than when it is replaced and differently rendered. Thus, to understand Spinoza philosophically demands a dual role and a dual function. It is necessary to learn his (philosophic) language and to use it in his manner.

It is equally necessary to become detached from him, and to appraise the (assertive) claims that he sets forth.

What a philosophic structure reveals does not necessarily square with what it affirms. This is to be expected, since the value of philosophic understanding is neither solely dependent upon nor solely reducible to a body of affirmative claims. But regardless of the ways in which the exhibitive and assertive functions of philosophy do and do not reinforce each other, they are always distinguishable. The history of philosophy, as everyone knows, is written sometimes in terms of problems, and sometimes in terms of systems. The "cultural" approach, and various others, bridge a gap between these two, trying to explain why new answers to old problems do not have to be incompatible with one another, and why new problems are always being born. The "systems" approach, much the simplest for the historian, has had its share of severe criticism, and for good reason. And yet it retains a certain residual validity: it is in a position to recognize the exhibitive function of a structure of ideas. Most important philosophers are undeniably involved in the problems of their predecessors. But it is remarkably easy to forget that they are interested equally in depicting just what they discern in the world, and just what impact the world has made on them, whether or not in so doing they resolve any previous perplexity or ameliorate anybody's intellectual plight.

Though philosophy shares the exhibitive function of utterance with art, the manner in which this function works itself out is not the same in philosophy as in the commonly identified arts. The exhibitive medium in philosophy remains conceptual; it is the framework of abstract concepts that ultimately performs the exhibitive function. The character and force of the function always depend in part upon the types of dramatic interplay that are to be found among the concepts, and upon the (communicative) devices by which the concepts are ordered for assimilation. The view that an exhibitive dimension is basic to philosophy must not be confounded with the stylish allegation that philosophy is to a large extent "non-cognitive." The exhibitive aspect of the discipline may be no less cognitive than the assertive. Any methodic deployment of natural complexes which stimulates further methodic activity of whatever kind may contribute knowledge that is far more than incidental. This condition and potentiality holds for all of the arts, and for each form of human utterance.

From the foregoing account it should be evident that philosophy cannot be interpreted solely in terms of the speculative reason as Whitehead understands it. But we may turn now to the contention that the philosophic or speculative reason is "untrammeled by method," and to the conception of philosophy as being unlike any other discipline in its attempt to "transcend all method." Whitehead's insistence upon the freedom and even the license of speculation, on the need for an unrestricted movement of the philosophic imagination, is a magnificent defiance: of timidity, which disguises itself as precision; of poverty, which disguises itself as rigor; and of narrowness, which builds its own scholasticism on provincial canons of legitimacy. Nevertheless, the problem of the relation between freedom and method calls for a number of distinctions. So far as the individual philosopher and his philosophic structure are concerned, it would be nonsense to suppose that no method is present. If the existence of a formal discipline and deliberate conceptual activity do not imply method, nothing else does. Whitehead concedes that speculative reason is "subject" to method; but it is futile to guess what he means. Now it is possible to argue that the philosopher, in the choice of his method, or in the number of basic methodological options available to him, has greater latitude than the scientist has. Yet his latitude is not greater than that of the artist. If the relative freedom of choice is what justifies the idea that the philosopher transcends method, the artist cannot be denied the same power. Could the notion of reason as "speculative" suggest that the philosopher does not really "choose" a method but that his method emerges as a natural order or habitation for his unrestricted imaginings? It is true that in most instances of original philosophic thought, specific methods emerge along with substantive activity, despite the prior presence of general methodic intent. But this is true as well of methodic areas other than philosophy; areas which we should not wish to regard as expressions of the "speculative."

Does the fact that the philosopher can examine his own method place him beyond any particular method? The scientist and the artist may reflect on their own methods, but not in the same methodic mode under which they pursue their proper discipline. The philosopher's examination of his own method actually may be part of his philosophic query, and may be continuous with the other issues of which it treats. The difference seems indisputable. But the process whereby a philosophic method examines itself does not necessarily diminish dependency upon that method. It may result in modification of the method. The method may open the way to steps culminating in its own metamorphosis. But the intermediate philosophic process, when it does not continue to depend upon the method that is being modified, depends upon some other method appropriately invoked. Every imaginative departure of query occurs in a controlled order of utterance. The chance insight or happy accident derives its ultimate relevancy from the environment in which it arose and in which it will take effect.

The historical succession of perspectives forces a somewhat different light on the relation between philosophy and method. Philosophies use different methods, even if philosophy uses an overarching method. The latter, elusive as it may be, is what justifies the making of comparisons among the many methods. Each of the "many" is concerned with the shaping of a constellation of ideas, and as a whole it is unique. The overarching "one," which remains influential even when disavowed or forgotten, is concerned with preserving the heart and spirit of the discipline. It is that method of judging which inevitably employs assertive and exhibitive functions toward a common end, to see and to distinguish, to grasp and to analyze, to frame and to formulate, to isolate and to group natural complexes as no other discipline wishes to or can. Now the many are collectively and historically responsible for the survival of the one: they provide it with new expressions of content and form. They are methodic embodiments of the primary methodic mandate—revivifications of the generic power (method) of philosophic judgment. Their number, let alone their collective value, discredits any claim for the sufficiency of a single mode of assertion and portrayal. They show each mode to be significant only in the society of other possible modes. If it is true that every philosophic outlook articulates a culture or an epoch, the meaning of rivalry among the many methods, both within an epoch and in different epochs, is considerably altered. Whatever the case may be, the accumulation of philosophic experience through the ages suggests that philosophy as a continuing discipline transcends any single method of embodying its spirit. Here, on the historical level, the analogy with art cannot be retained. The various methods in art are all directed toward the exhibitive manipulation of natural complexes. Each is self-sufficient in so far as its contrivances need not justify it critically and conceptually. But philosophy is required by its assertive dimension to defend as well as to contrive and show.

A philosophy seeks more than its method can yield. At least implicitly, and often in contrast to its direct intentions, it acknowledges other, different philosophies; an acknowledgment which consists not in the expression of piety or historical decorum, but in genuine connection. This is the essential meaning in the old saw that philosophic problems are never solved. They cannot be univocally determined in the way that scientific problems are. When dealing with problems, the philosopher, like the scientist, takes some things for granted. But owing partly to the exhibitive dimension of his procedure, it is difficult for him to share fully with other philosophers the sense of what are the best things to be taken for granted. If he lives long enough and sees himself from enough of a distance, he becomes doubtful about his own original choices. Philosophic methods, then, are transcended by philosophic aims. Whatever the consequences may be for "intelligence," the philosopher is unable to adjust means to ends with any semblance of the definitiveness attained in other forms of discipline. Much of this travail of imbalance and insecurity he can spare himself, by lowering his sights, purging his discipline of its extravagant hopes, and confining himself to problems not more docile, perhaps, but more bountiful of reward. The alternative is to endure his identity, which is molded by his deeper feelings, and to accept the methodic lameness he has inherited, since he must perceive sooner or later that the beauty and the meaning of his query are unimpaired.

Notes

1. M. R. Cohen, article "Method, Scientific" in *Encyclo-paedia of the Social Sciences* (New York, 1933).
2. The quotations from Jeremy Bentham are taken from the *Essay on Logic* (mss. 1811–1831), Chapters I, II, VI, IX, X, and Appendices A and B. Additional material on which the presentation of his views is based comes from: *Chrestomathia* (1816), Appendix IV, section VII, heading II, with footnotes; and *A Fragment on Ontology* (mss. 1813–1821), Chapter I. All of these are in Bentham's *Works*, Vol. VIII, edited by John Bowring (Edinburgh, 1843).
3. The quotations from S. T. Coleridge and the material on which the presentation of his views is based are taken from: *A Preliminary Treatise on Method*, or General Introduction of The Encyclopaedia Metropolitana (1818), edited by Alice D. Snyder as *Coleridge's Treatise on Method* (London, 1934); and *The Friend* (1818), Section 2, Essays iv–xi, collectively entitled "Principles of the Science of Method," in *Complete Works*, edited by W. G. T. Shedd (New York, 1843). Many of the passages quoted from the *Preliminary Treatise* also appear either verbatim or with minor verbal changes in *The Friend*.
4. The translation of the *Regulae* here used is mainly that of Elizabeth Haldane and G. R. T. Ross, *Philosophical Works of Descartes* (Cambridge, England, 1911, 1931), but at times that of N. Kemp Smith, *Descartes' Philosophical Writings* (London, 1952). For the occasional feeling of a

key term, the original (in C. Adam and P. Tannery, *Oeuvres de Descartes,* Vol. X, Paris, 1908) is useful even for bungling non-Latinists.

5. Unless otherwise specified, all quotations from John Dewey are from his *The Quest for Certainty,* Chapters VIII and IX (New York, 1929).

6. Francis Bacon, *The Advancement of Learning,* edited by G. W. Kitchin, Everyman's Library (London, 1915).

7. All quotations from A. N. Whitehead are from his *The Function of Reason* (Princeton, 1929).

8. John Locke, *An Essay Concerning Human Understanding,* II, xxi, 3.

9. Thomas Hobbes, *Elements of Philosophy Concerning Body (De Corpore),* Chapter VI.

10. Bacon, *The Advancement of Learning,* Everyman ed., pp. 140–141.

11. Sigmund Freud, *Civilization and its Discontents* (London, 1930), p. 36.

12. See note 5 above.

13. John Dewey, *Logic: The Theory of Inquiry* (New York, 1938), p. 9.

14. John Dewey, *Philosophy and Civilization* (New York, 1931), p. 78.

15. John Dewey, *Experience and Nature* (2d ed., New York, 1929), p. 134.

16. Dewey, *Logic,* p. 9.

17. See note 7 above.

18. Bacon, *The Advancement of Learning,* Everyman ed., p. 32.

19. *Ibid.,* p. 142.

INDEX

Abstraction, 12 ff., 22, 30
Accident, 40
Action, 12, 29, 68, 94, 128, 137, 142, 144, 166
Activity, 2, 7, 18, 38, 40, 42, 59, 65 f., 88, 101, 105, 135-44 *passim*, 162, 169
Adventure, 34, 157 f.
Aim, 49, 87, 90, 110, 141
Anselm, 64
Anticipation, 34, 40, 53, 77, 107, 139
Aphorisms, 161 f.
Apollonian, 64
Application, 1 ff., 16, 132 f.
Appraisal, 97
Aquinas, 119, 121, 165
Arbitrary, 21, 133
Arrangement, 9 ff., 15-35 *passim*, 36, 55
Art, 12 ff., 22, 28 f., 32 f., 37, 47, 51, 85, 98, 110, 114, 118, 120 f., 128 ff., 143, 149, 153 f., 164-72 *passim*
Articulation, 129-34
Assertion, 57, 93 f., 99, 117, 123, 127, 137, 166, 169
Assimilation, 89, 92, 169
Attention, 30
Audacity, 111 f.
Availability, 3 f., 96, 130

Bach, 51
Bacon, Francis, 40, 82, 136, 161 f.
Balance, 37 f., 62 ff.
Balzac, 120

Bentham, 9-35, 42, 46, 48, 54 f., 61, 69, 83, 95

Chance, 14, 30 f., 33, 74, 83 ff.
Choice, 150 ff.
Circumstances, 32 f., 73, 107, 112, 139
Clarification, 134
Classification, 29
Cohen, M. R., 1-8
Coleridge, 36-68, 69, 71 f., 83, 113, 163
Combination, 15, 21, 30, 69
Communication, 23 ff., 119
Conception, 39 f.
Concepts, 123 f., 165 ff.
Conclusions, 56
Configuration, 10, 24
Connected aggregation, 10 ff., 17, 27 f., 61
Conscience, 45, 67 f.
Consummation, 18, 35, 38, 48, 57, 95, 114
Contingency, 85
Continuity, 36, 57 ff.
Contrivance, 94, 128, 137, 142 ff., 166
Control, 34 f., 77, 84, 96, 107
Correctness, 69, 106
Criticism, 102, 131
Critique of Pure Reason, 86

Decision, 132 f.
Deduction, 70, 78, 121
Delacroix, 64
Delivery, 136

Descartes, 64, 69-86, 122, 140
Determinateness, 95, 108, 146, 149, 154
Determination, 129, 133
Device, 1, 71, 169
Dewey, John, 81 f., 138, 140, 145-54, 155 ff.
Dickinson, Emily, 64
Dionysian, 64
Direction, 79, 83, 85 f., 113 ff., 144
Discipline, 35, 99, 163, 173
Discourse, 9 ff., 19 ff., 29, 61, 79, 98, 131, 133
Discourse on Method, 69, 80
Discovery, 13, 30, 37, 40, 84
Discretion, 71, 74, 113, 140
Disraeli, 64
Distinctness, 8, 10, 20 f., 26, 49 f.
Diversity, 1, 7, 53, 72, 138, 163
Doing, 56, 94, 103, 116 f.
Dominion, 112

Economy, 54 f., 71, 109 f., 161
Education, 44
Effects, 132 ff.
Eliot, T. S., 64
Ends, 16 ff., 30, 42, 102, 104 f., 107-11, 113, 115, 133, 135-44 *passim*, 150 ff., 159
Enlightenment, 46
Entities, 7, 11, 17, 20, 25, 95
Estimation, 67 f., 97, 147, 149, 153 f.
Ethics, 12 ff.
Euclid's *Elements*, 36, 60
Exhibitive utterance, 94, 137, 165 ff.
Expectation, 4, 21, 48, 110, 135
Experience, 23
Experiment, 40, 54

Facilitation, 108 f.
Familiarity, 15
Feeling, 37, 41
Fictitious, 10, 17, 95
Freud, 143
Friend, The, 44 f.
Function, 93 f.

Gain, 92 f.
Gargantua and *Pantagruel*, 110
Giotto, 64
Good, 142 f., 146, 156 ff.

Groping, 48, 83 ff.
Grouping, 17, 20 f.
Guiding idea, 39, 48, 50 ff., 71
Guiding principle, 97

Habit, 43, 112-14, 159
Hamlet, 38, 60, 62, 64
Hamlet, 60
Hegel, 64, 165
Heidegger, 121
Hitler, 147 ff.
Hobbes, 109
Human, 12, 22, 47, 91, 94, 97, 112, 132 f., 137, 141, 143, 155, 160 f.
Human Comedy, 120
Hume, 64
Hypothesis, 39

Ibsen, 120
Idea, 4, 11, 39 f., 50 ff., 100, 166
Imagination, 12 ff., 22, 30, 41, 106, 114, 169 ff.
Impression, 37, 44, 62 f., 65
Individual, 91, 137, 144
Industrial method, 72 f., 113
Initiative, 39 ff., 50, 52 f.
Innocent III, 64
Inquiry, 54, 105, 128, 142 f., 149
Inspiration, 43, 71, 156, 163 f.
Instinct, 40 f.
Instrument, 13, 30, 61, 100, 103 f.
Intellect, 41, 43, 55
Intellectualism, 55, 87
Intelligence, 81 ff., 140, 145-54 *passim*, 155 f., 173
Intention, 76 f., 91 f., 108, 119 f.
Interrogative temper, 85, 114 f., 143
Intuition, 70, 78-80, 165
Invention, 4, 12 ff., 18, 22 f., 30 ff., 54, 61, 72, 83, 85, 105, 108, 111 f., 114, 143, 159

James, William, 67
Judgment, 12, 67 f., 92 ff., 114, 137, 165 ff.; *see also* Utterance

Kant, 86–88, 121
Kierkegaard, 119, 122
Knowledge, 64, 69, 82, 116-17, 133, 136, 157, 161 ff., 169

Language, 167
Law, 38 f., 43, 64, 73, 95
Leading idea, *see* Guiding idea
Leibniz, 119
Life, 41 f., 156 ff.
Literature, 39 f.
Locke, 101
Logic, 12 ff., 29, 126 ff.
Luck, 65, 84

Madame Bovary, 110
Making, 56, 94, 103, 116 f.
Manipulation, 57, 60, 89, 92 ff., 99, 104, 110, 135-44 *passim*, 152, 166
Mastery, 112
Materials, 15, 26 f., 37, 89, 100, 143
Mathematics, 54, 63, 109, 118, 160
Matisse, 64
Mean, 37 f., 44, 62 ff.
Meaning, 51, 77, 132 ff., 160, 166
Means, 102 ff., 115, 145-54 *passim*
Memory, 12, 22
Meno, 36, 57 ff.
Methodography, 128 f., 131
Methodolatry, 105 f.
Methodology, 124-29, 131, 156
Methodos, 2, 36
Michelangelo, 121
Moby Dick, 84
Moore, G. E., 165
Movement, 36, 42, 46
Mozart, 120
Mrs. Quickly, 38, 64
Music, 65, 160

Names, 11
Napoleon, 64
Natural complex, 7, 21 f., 54, 84, 89 ff., 123, 135 ff., 160, 166 f.
Nature, 41, 84, 93 f., 112, 146
Necessity, 38
Need, 90, 110
Nietzsche, 119, 121
Novelty, 138, 157 ff.

Object, 1, 4, 6 ff., 9 ff., 15-35 *passim*, 61
Objectivity, 133
Observation, 13, 15, 29 f., 161 f.
Operation, 2, 12, 22 f., 40, 78, 102, 118, 132, 146, 157

Order, 1 ff., 15, 20, 42, 60, 69 f., 74 f., 96 f., 101, 117, 132, 135-44 *passim*, 165
Oresteia, 120

Part, 10, 24, 26, 48, 53, 61, 105
Particular, 39, 44, 82
Passion, 41
Passivity, 37 f., 43
Path, 2 f., 36, 70, 114
Pattern, 1, 3 ff., 17, 39, 102, 114, 119 f., 133
Peirce, C. S., 119
Perception, 12, 23
Perfection, 81, 91, 142
Pericles, 64
Perspective, 48, 60, 68, 77, 96 f., 101, 137-38, 140, 166
Philosophic method, 20 f., 28, 37, 98 f., 121-24, 128, 132-34, 149, 164-73
Philosophy, 51, 55, 85, 109, 114, 119, 124 f., 130, 153 f., 163-73
Physical, 11, 20
Plan, 50, 53, 59, 68
Plato, 43 f., 50 f., 58, 64, 72, 119
Plotinus, 122
Poetry, 41, 43, 131, 160
Policy, 73, 81 ff., 125
Portrayal, 123, 167
Position, 92
Possibility, 100, 135, 147, 153 f.
Power, 89, 93, 99-102, 104 f., 114, 117, 126, 135-44 *passim*
Practice, 12, 29, 32
Preconception, 39 f., 55
Predictability, 3, 15, 17 f., 74
Prescription, 32, 69, 76
Principle, 59, 86-88, 127, 132
Prior and posterior, 10, 27 f., 52 f.
Problem, 50, 54, 122, 146-54 *passim*
Procedure, 1-3, 52 ff.
Process, 2, 28, 105, 133
Product, 66, 91, 94 f., 102 ff., 118 ff., 139 ff., 166
Progression, 36, 39, 57, 59 ff.
Proposal, 54, 57
Proposition, 55, 57, 86 ff., 165
Protagoras, 64
Prudence, 19, 153
Psychical, 11, 20

Purpose, 6, 16, 32, 40, 42, 48, 50, 56, 72, 74, 83 f., 87, 99 f., 103, 107-14 *passim*, 135-44 *passim*, 161

Query, 85, 105, 114 f., 141, 142-44, 165, 171
Quickly, Mrs., 38, 64

Racine, 64
Randomness, 19, 83 f.
Rational, 1, 5 ff., 55, 83, 157 f.
Rationale, 125, 129
Real, 11, 17, 25, 45, 129, 135 f.
Reason, 69, 71, 80, 114, 141, 155-70 *passim*
Rectitude, 30
Reflection, 38, 62 f.
Regularity, 15, 17 f., 34, 72, 74
Relatedness, 20
Relation, 37 f., 101, 123
Religion, 41, 45, 114, 155
Remedy, 18, 27, 46, 90
Repeatability, 2 f., 17, 19, 54, 72, 89, 91, 96, 102 f., 114, 159 ff.
Reproducible order, 16, 97, 112, 135-44 *passim*
Resolution, 76, 133 f.
Result, 17 f., 32 f., 49, 59, 105, 107 ff., 119 f., 122, 126, 159, 162
Rhythm, 140-41
Romanticism, 46
Rule, 2, 4, 69-82 *passim*, 95, 100, 121, 128, 134, 136, 140
Rules for the Direction of the Mind, 69

Saying, 93, 103, 116 f.
Science, 12 ff., 22, 29, 37, 39, 42, 45, 51 ff., 64, 85, 97, 109, 114, 119, 127, 130, 143, 153 f., 155 ff., 163 ff.
Scientific method, 20 f., 28, 35, 42, 52 ff., 96 ff., 104 f., 125 f., 128, 132 f., 153, 155 f., 170, 172
Sculpture, 61
Sectarianism, 142 ff.
Selection, 67
Sense, 37, 40
Sequence, 53, 58, 61, 118 f., 121 f.
Shakespeare, 43, 51, 64, 72, 163 f.
Showing, 165 ff.

Signs, 11, 25, 99, 137, 149, 160, 166 f.
Sistine chapel, 120 f.
Situation, 149 ff.
Socrates, 36, 118 f.
Spinoza, 119, 121, 167
Stages, 60 f.
Stalin, 64
Standardization, 130
Statement, 94
Steps, 2, 36, 77 f.
Stratagem, 4
Strategy, 91, 125, 127
Strindberg, 64
Structure, 28, 43, 48, 53
Successive exhibition, 10 ff., 17, 27 f., 61
System, 1, 5 ff., 41 ff., 51, 70 ff., 118-24, 162, 168

Tactic, 12, 32, 34 f., 96
Technique, 1, 34, 54, 96 ff., 128
Technology, 18, 35, 132 f.
Theory, 38 f., 47, 103, 125, 137
Thought, 12, 29, 37, 41, 50
Tolstoy, 64
Trade, 40, 56
Tradition, 142 f.
Transition, 36, 58
Translation, 133, 135 ff.
Triviality, 5
Truth-seeking, 7, 36 ff., 55 f., 69, 99

Understanding, 45, 156, 168
Unification, 43, 47, 49, 57
Unique, 46, 53 f., 75, 112, 129, 165 ff.
Unity, 36, 39, 43, 47 ff., 60
Universal, 39, 44, 82, 100, 114, 128
Utterance, 55, 57, 92, 94 ff., 114, 128, 135-44 *passim*, 166, 168 f.; *see also* Judgment

Vagueness, 76, 83, 85, 108
Vision, 49, 55, 71

Way, 2, 36, 53, 70 f., 79 ff., 96, 102 f., 142, 144
Whitehead, 90, 140, 155-70
Whole, 53, 105
Will, 45, 67
Wycherley, 64